T0191156

NATIONAL GEOGRAPHIC
KiDS

BEGINNER'S
UNITED STATES
ATLAS

NATIONAL GEOGRAPHIC
WASHINGTON, D.C.

Contents

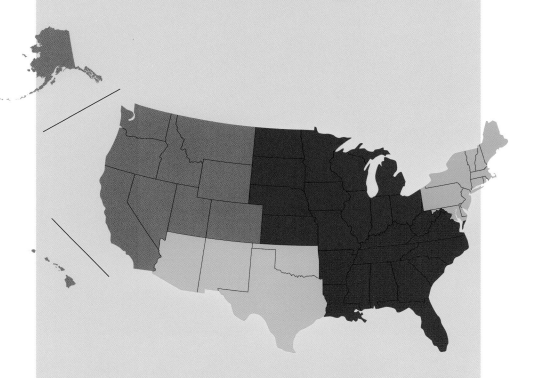

Learning the Basics

This atlas uses maps and photographs to show the many differences in the people, animals, and places that make up the United States. The atlas divides the country into five regions, each indicated by a different color, as shown on the map above. The introduction to each region includes a locator map that highlights the states of the region in yellow.

What Is a Map?

An atlas is a collection of maps and pictures. A map is a drawing of a place as it looks from above. It is flat, and it is smaller than the place it shows. Learning to read a map can help you find where you are and where you want to go. Maps in this atlas are simplified to help you read them.

Mapping your home ...

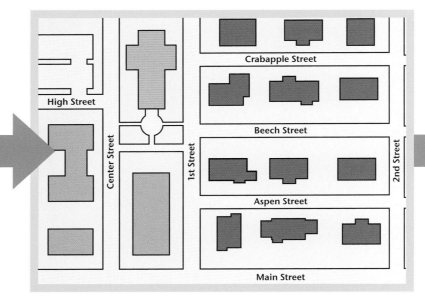

From a bird's-eye view ...
you would see only the tops of things, just as a bird flying directly overhead would. You wouldn't see walls, tree trunks, tires, or feet.

On a large-scale map ...
you see places from a bird's-eye view. But a map uses drawings called symbols to show things on the ground, such as houses or streets. The map of the National Mall in Washington, D.C., on pages 10–11 is an example of a large-scale map.

Finding places on the map

A map can help you get where you want to go.
A map includes a compass rose, a scale,
and a key to help you read the map.

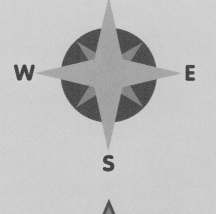

A compass rose helps you travel in the right direction. It tells you where north (N), south (S), east (E), and west (W) are on your map.

Often only a north arrow is used.

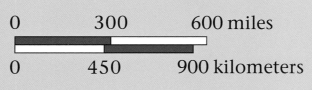

A scale tells you about distance on a map. The scale shows what length on the map represents the labeled distance on the ground.

On an intermediate-scale map …

you see a place from much higher up. A town appears as a tiny dot. You can't see houses, but you can see more of the land around the town. Most maps in this atlas show a whole state with its towns and cities and other special features.

On a small-scale map …

you can see much more of the country around a state, including other states. But on a small-scale map there is much less detail. You can no longer see most features within the state. Two states—Alaska and Hawai'i—are often shown in separate boxes or on a map of the whole continent, as on pages 6–7.

A map key helps you understand the symbols used by the mapmaker to show things like cities, rivers, boundaries, forests, and points of interest on the map.

Map Key for the State Maps in This Atlas

- • Aspen ....*town of under 25,000 residents*
- • Frankfort ....*town of 25,000 to 99,999*
- • San Jose ....*city of 100,000 to 999,999*
- • **New York** ....*city of 1,000,000 and over*

⚛   National capital

★   State capital

▪   Point of interest

•••••   Country boundary

·········   State boundary

·········   Continental Divide

+   High point

▾   Low point

////   Area below sea level

⎯⎯   River

⎯⎯   Lake

▦   Dry lake

⎯⎯   Swamp

▨   Glacier

▭   Indian Reservation (I.R.)
All Indian Reservations are not shown due to map scale and reservation size.

▭   National Park (N.P.)

▭   National Forest land

THE LAND
The Physical United States

LAND REGIONS The rugged Sierra Nevada and Rocky Mountains run north to south through the western United States. Between these mountains are dry lands with little vegetation. East of the Rockies are wide, grassy plains and the older, lower Appalachian Mountains.

WATER Together, the Mississippi and the Missouri form the longest river system in the United States. The Great Lakes are the largest freshwater lakes in the country.

CLIMATE The United States has many climate types—from cold Alaska to tropical Hawai'i, with milder climates in the other 48 states.

PLANTS The United States has forests where there is plenty of rain. Grasslands cover drier areas.

ANIMALS There are many kinds of animals—everything from bears and deer to songbirds large and small.

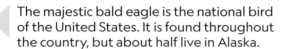

The majestic bald eagle is the national bird of the United States. It is found throughout the country, but about half live in Alaska.

Deserts are found in the southwestern part of the United States. This large rock formation is in Monument Valley in Utah.

North America is famous for its deciduous forests. Leaves turn fiery colors each fall.

PACIFIC OCEAN

Moloka'i

Hawai'i

Waves off the Pacific Ocean roll onto a beach along the shore of Moloka'i, one of the islands that make up the state of Hawai'i.

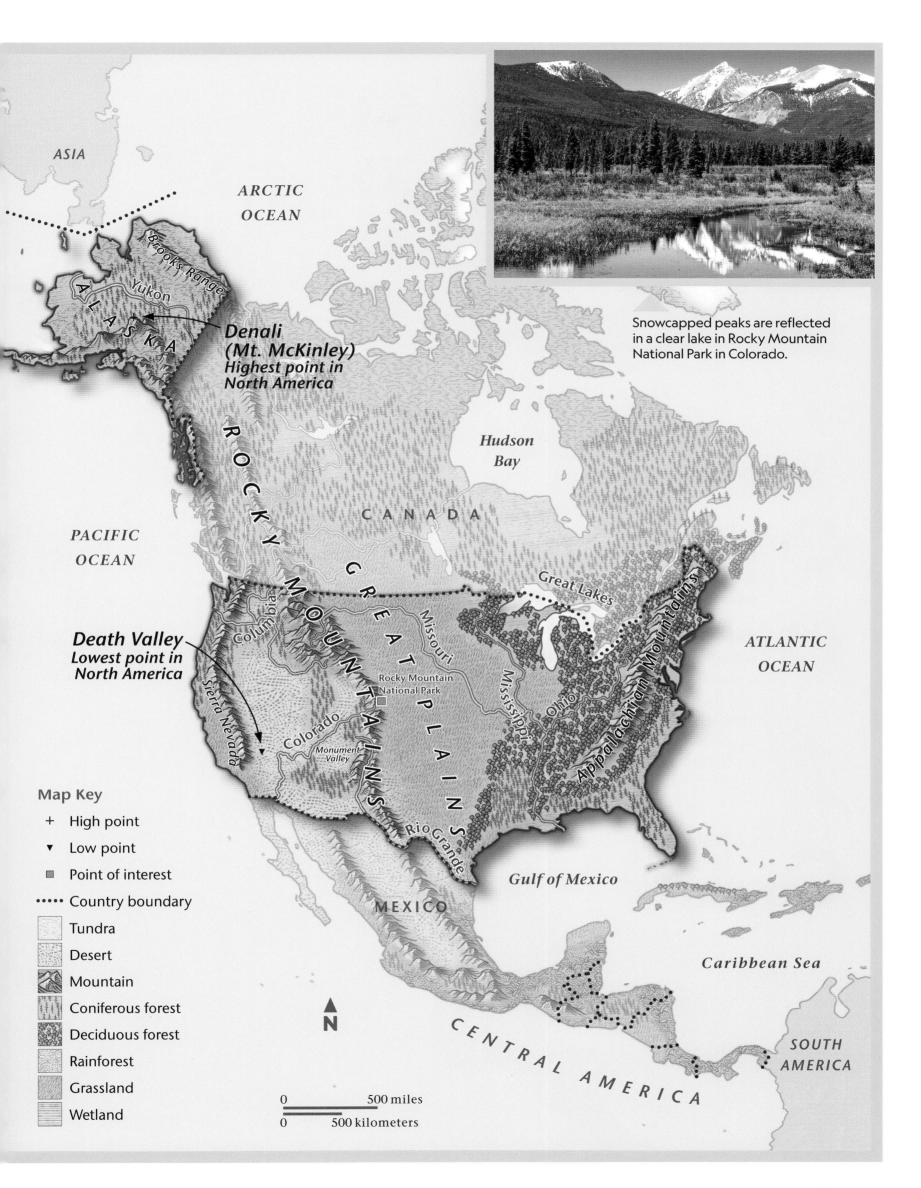

ASIA

ARCTIC
OCEAN

Brooks Range

ALASKA

Yukon

**Denali
(Mt. McKinley)**
Highest point in
North America

PACIFIC
OCEAN

CANADA

Hudson
Bay

Snowcapped peaks are reflected
in a clear lake in Rocky Mountain
National Park in Colorado.

R O C K Y   M O U N T A I N S

Columbia

Death Valley
Lowest point in
North America

Sierra Nevada

Colorado

Monument
Valley

G R E A T   P L A I N S

Missouri

Mississippi

Rocky Mountain
National Park

Great Lakes

Ohio

Appalachian Mountains

ATLANTIC
OCEAN

Rio Grande

Gulf of Mexico

MEXICO

Caribbean Sea

Map Key

+ High point

▼ Low point

■ Point of interest

•••• Country boundary

Tundra

Desert

Mountain

Coniferous forest

Deciduous forest

Rainforest

Grassland

Wetland

N

C E N T R A L   A M E R I C A

SOUTH
AMERICA

0   500 miles

0   500 kilometers

THE PEOPLE
The Political United States

 STATES The United States is made up of 50 states. Alaska and Hawai'i are separated from the rest of the country. So you can see them close up, they are shown here in the Pacific Ocean south of the state of California.

CITIES Washington, D.C., is the national capital. Each state has its own capital. New York City has the most people of any U.S. city.

PEOPLE The United States is made up of people from all over the world and descendants of the native people who first lived on this land. Most live and work in and around cities. In this atlas, city proper and state population figures are from 2018 unless otherwise noted.

LANGUAGES English is the main language, followed by Spanish.

Baseball is a popular sport in the United States, along with soccer, basketball, and football.

Chinese New Year is a big celebration in San Francisco. Many Chinese Americans live in this California city.

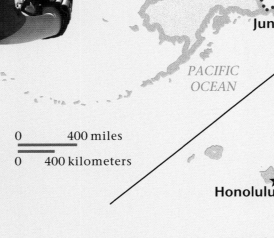

0 — 400 miles
0 — 400 kilometers

0 — 150 miles
0 — 150 kilometers

PACIFIC OCEAN

ALASKA

Juneau

PACIFIC OCEAN

PACIFIC OCEAN

HAWAI'I

Honolulu

Seattle
Olympia
WASHINGTON
Portland
Salem
OREGON
IDAHO
Helena
MO
Boise
Carson City
Salt Lake City
Sacramento
CALIFORNIA
NEVADA
UTAH
San Francisco
San Jose
Las Vegas
Colorado
ARIZONA
Los Angeles
Phoenix
San Diego
Tucson

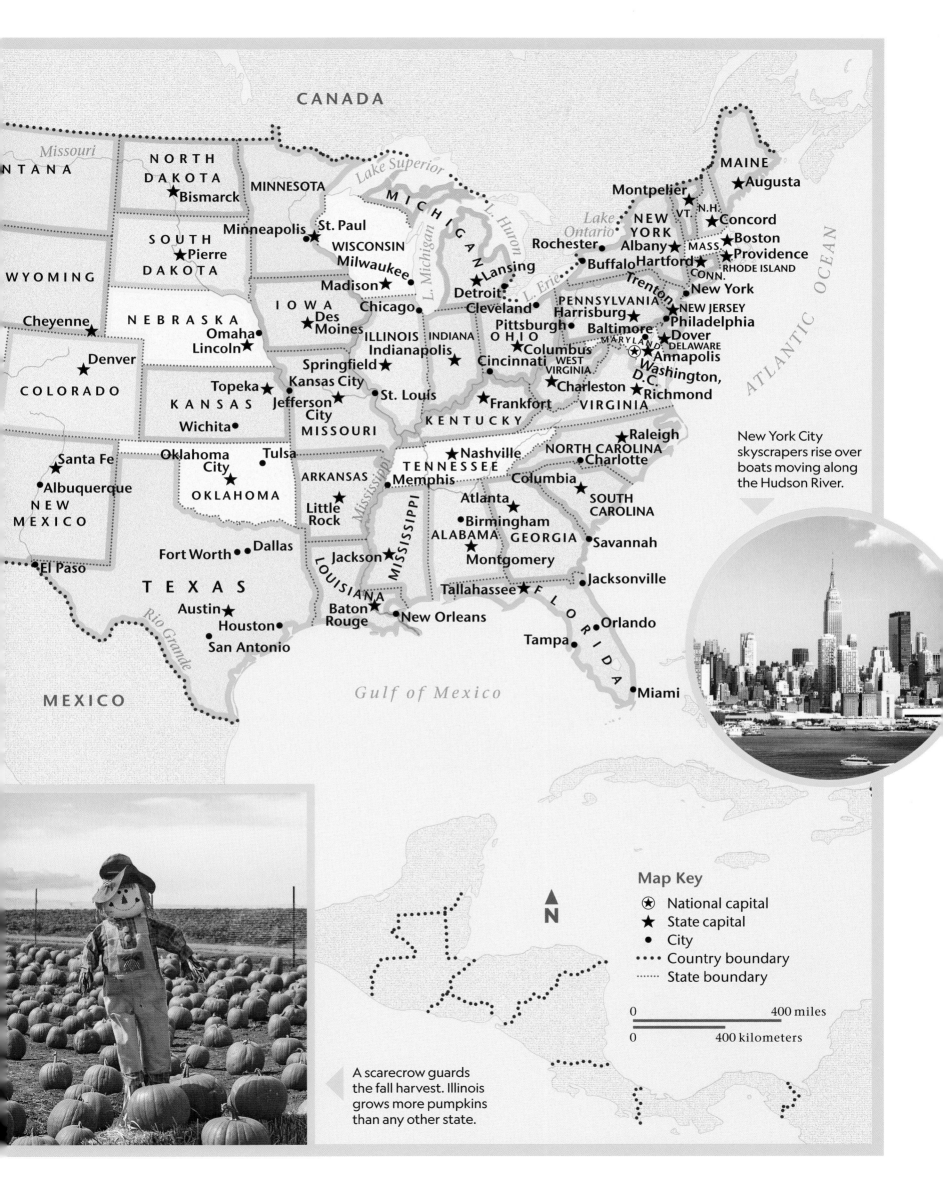

CANADA

Missouri

NTANA

WYOMING

Cheyenne ★

Denver ★

COLORADO

Santa Fe ★
• Albuquerque
NEW
MEXICO

• El Paso

T E X A S

Fort Worth • • Dallas

Austin ★
• Houston
San Antonio •

Rio Grande

MEXICO

NORTH
DAKOTA
★ Bismarck

MINNESOTA

Minneapolis • • St. Paul

SOUTH
DAKOTA
Pierre ★

NEBRASKA

Omaha •
Lincoln ★

Des
Moines ★

I O W A

WISCONSIN

Milwaukee
Madison ★

ILLINOIS

Springfield ★

Topeka ★ • Kansas City

Jefferson ★
City
Wichita •

K A N S A S

MISSOURI

• St. Louis

Oklahoma ★ • Tulsa
City

OKLAHOMA

Little ★
Rock

ARKANSAS

Lake Superior

MICHIGAN

Lansing ★

Chicago •

Detroit •

INDIANA

Indianapolis ★

L. Michigan

L. Huron

*Lake
Ontario*

NEW
YORK

Rochester •
Albany ★

Buffalo •

L. Erie

Cleveland •

OHIO

Columbus ★

Cincinnati •

Frankfort ★

K E N T U C K Y

Nashville ★

T E N N E S S E E

Memphis •

Mississippi

Jackson ★

MISSISSIPPI

LOUISIANA

Baton ★
Rouge

• New Orleans

Atlanta ★

• Birmingham

ALABAMA

Montgomery ★

PENNSYLVANIA
Harrisburg ★
Pittsburgh •

Trenton ★

NEW JERSEY

Baltimore •
MARYLAND
Annapolis ★
WEST
VIRGINIA

Charleston ★

VIRGINIA

Raleigh ★

NORTH CAROLINA
Charlotte •

Columbia ★

SOUTH
CAROLINA

Savannah •

GEORGIA

Tallahassee ★

Jacksonville •

F L O R I D A

Orlando •

Tampa •

Miami •

MAINE
★ Augusta

Montpelier ★
VT. N.H.
★ Concord

★ Boston
MASS. ★ Providence
Hartford ★
CONN. RHODE ISLAND

New York •

Philadelphia •

Dover ★
DELAWARE

Washington,
D.C.
Richmond ★

Gulf of Mexico

ATLANTIC
OCEAN

New York City
skyscrapers rise over
boats moving along
the Hudson River.

Map Key

⊛ National capital

★ State capital

• City

••• Country boundary

··· State boundary

| 0 | 400 miles |

| 0 | 400 kilometers |

A scarecrow guards
the fall harvest. Illinois
grows more pumpkins
than any other state.

N

THE NATIONAL CAPITAL
The District of Columbia

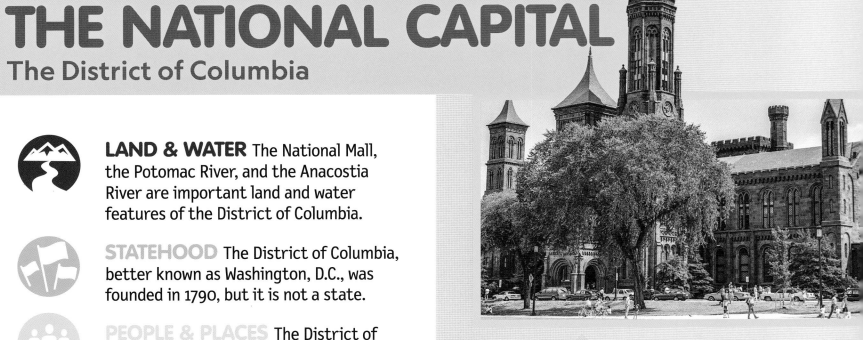

 LAND & WATER The National Mall, the Potomac River, and the Anacostia River are important land and water features of the District of Columbia.

 STATEHOOD The District of Columbia, better known as Washington, D.C., was founded in 1790, but it is not a state.

 PEOPLE & PLACES The District of Columbia's population is 702,455. The city is the seat of the U.S. government.

 FUN FACT The flag of the District of Columbia, with three red stars and two red stripes, is based on the shield in George Washington's family coat of arms.

The Smithsonian Institution, the world's largest museum, is actually made up of 19 museums and the National Zoo. Established in 1846, it is sometimes called the nation's attic because of its large collections.

Abraham Lincoln, who was president during the Civil War and a strong opponent of slavery, is remembered in a memorial that houses this seated statue at the west end of the National Mall.

Washington, D.C. Flag

American Beauty Rose
Official Flower

Wood Thrush
Official Bird

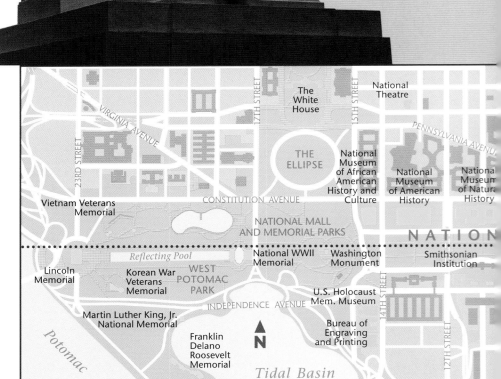

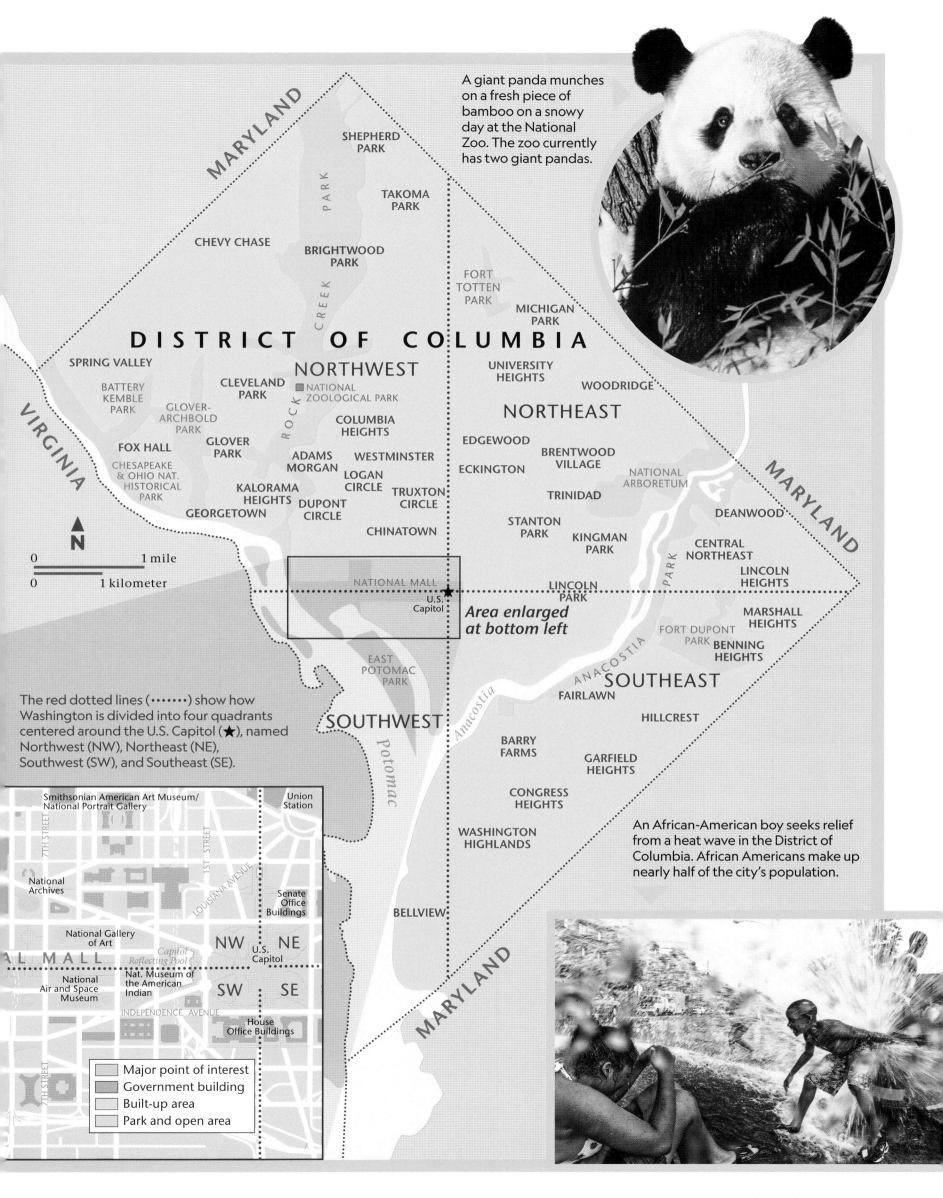

A giant panda munches on a fresh piece of bamboo on a snowy day at the National Zoo. The zoo currently has two giant pandas.

DISTRICT OF COLUMBIA

MARYLAND

VIRGINIA

MARYLAND

MARYLAND

SHEPHERD PARK

TAKOMA PARK

CHEVY CHASE

BRIGHTWOOD PARK

CREEK PARK

FORT TOTTEN PARK

MICHIGAN PARK

NORTHWEST

SPRING VALLEY

BATTERY KEMBLE PARK

GLOVER-ARCHBOLD PARK

CLEVELAND PARK

NATIONAL ZOOLOGICAL PARK

ROCK CREEK PARK

COLUMBIA HEIGHTS

UNIVERSITY HEIGHTS

WOODRIDGE

NORTHEAST

FOX HALL

GLOVER PARK

CHESAPEAKE & OHIO NAT. HISTORICAL PARK

ADAMS MORGAN

WESTMINSTER

EDGEWOOD

ECKINGTON

BRENTWOOD VILLAGE

NATIONAL ARBORETUM

KALORAMA HEIGHTS

LOGAN CIRCLE

TRINIDAD

GEORGETOWN

DUPONT CIRCLE

TRUXTON CIRCLE

STANTON PARK

KINGMAN PARK

DEANWOOD

CHINATOWN

CENTRAL NORTHEAST

LINCOLN HEIGHTS

NATIONAL MALL

LINCOLN PARK

U.S. Capitol

MARSHALL HEIGHTS

Area enlarged at bottom left

FORT DUPONT PARK

BENNING HEIGHTS

EAST POTOMAC PARK

ANACOSTIA PARK

SOUTHEAST

FAIRLAWN

HILLCREST

SOUTHWEST

Anacostia

BARRY FARMS

GARFIELD HEIGHTS

CONGRESS HEIGHTS

Potomac

WASHINGTON HIGHLANDS

The red dotted lines (••••••) show how Washington is divided into four quadrants centered around the U.S. Capitol (★), named Northwest (NW), Northeast (NE), Southwest (SW), and Southeast (SE).

BELLVIEW

An African-American boy seeks relief from a heat wave in the District of Columbia. African Americans make up nearly half of the city's population.

Smithsonian American Art Museum/ National Portrait Gallery

Union Station

7TH STREET

1ST STREET

LOUISIANA AVENUE

National Archives

National Gallery of Art

Capitol Reflecting Pool

Senate Office Buildings

NATIONAL MALL

NW

NE

U.S. Capitol

National Air and Space Museum

Nat. Museum of the American Indian

SW

SE

INDEPENDENCE AVENUE

House Office Buildings

7TH STREET

Major point of interest

Government building

Built-up area

Park and open area

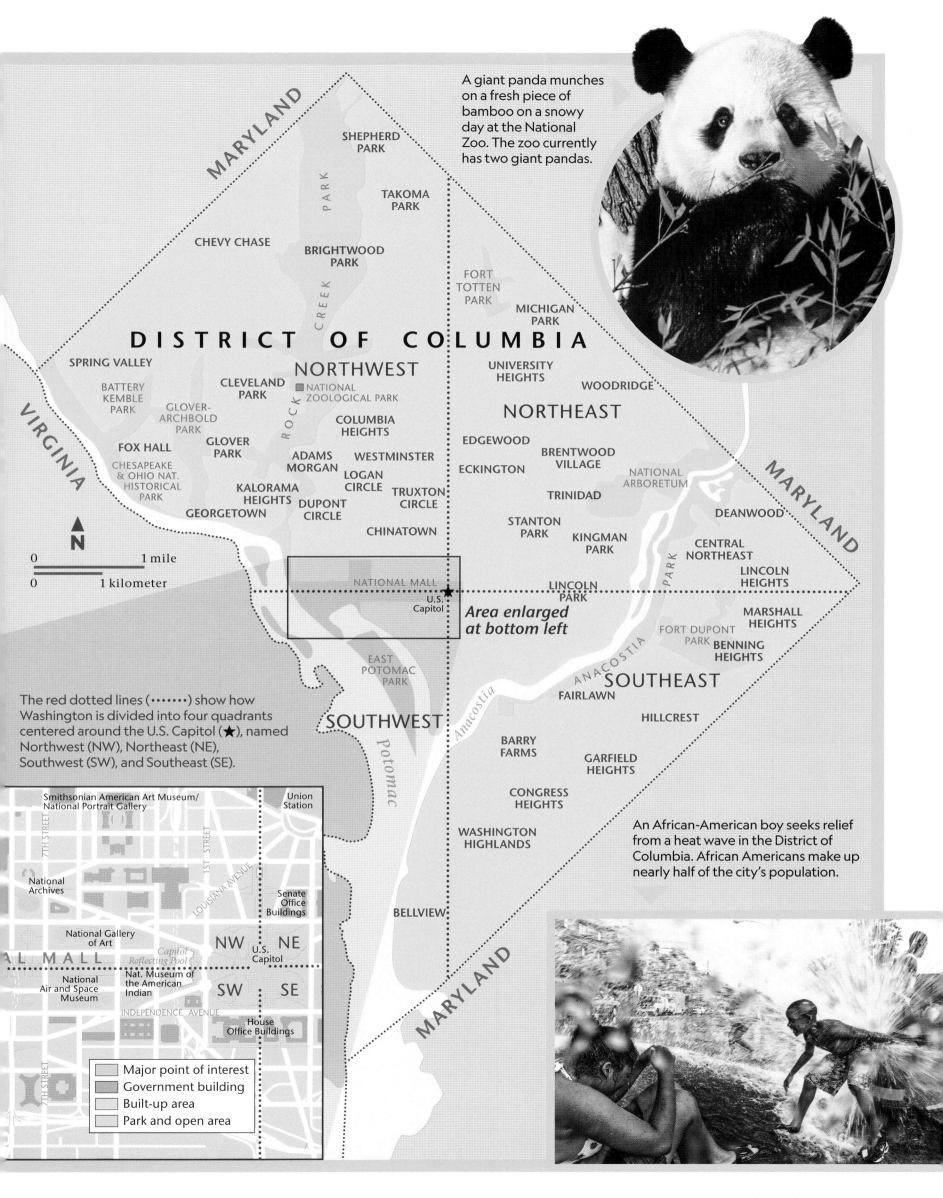

THE NORTHEAST

The earliest inhabitants of the river valleys and woodlands of the Northeast were Native American. Settlers and traders arrived from Europe and established colonies that eventually became states. Today people come from countries around the world to live here, bringing with them customs, languages, and beliefs that make the Northeast a region of great diversity. The region includes the country's financial center, New York City, and its political capital, Washington, D.C.

Black bears live throughout much of the United States, including the forests of the Northeast. Their diet includes roots, berries, and human garbage.

Water plunges as much as 110 feet (34 m) over the American Falls on the Niagara River near New York's northwestern border with the country of Canada.

CONNECTICUT

CONNECTICUT

 LAND & WATER Mount Frissell, the Connecticut River, and Long Island Sound are important land and water features of Connecticut.

 STATEHOOD Connecticut became the 5th state in 1788.

 PEOPLE & PLACES Connecticut's population is 3,572,665. Hartford is the state capital. The largest city is Bridgeport.

 FUN FACT The sperm whale, Connecticut's state animal, is known for its massive head. Its brain is larger than that of any other creature known to have lived on Earth.

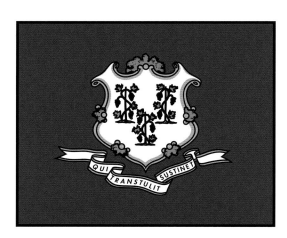

Connecticut State Flag

Mountain Laurel
State Flower

Robin
State Bird

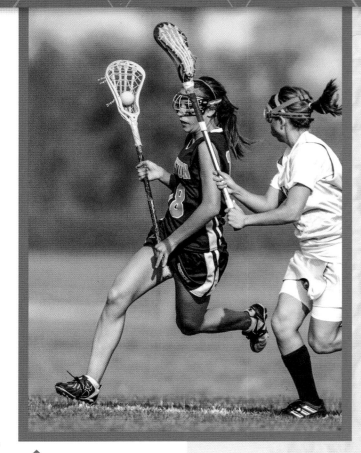

Lacrosse is a popular sport in schools and colleges in Connecticut and across the United States. It was derived from a game played by many Eastern Woodland Native Americans.

Mt. Frisse
2,380 ft
725 m

Highest poin in Connecticu

Taconic Range

Housatonic

New
Milford

Lake
Candlewood

NEW YORK

Danbury

N

Norwalk

Stamford

The *Charles W. Morgan,* launched in 1841 and now docked in Mystic Seaport, is the only remaining wooden whaling ship in the world.

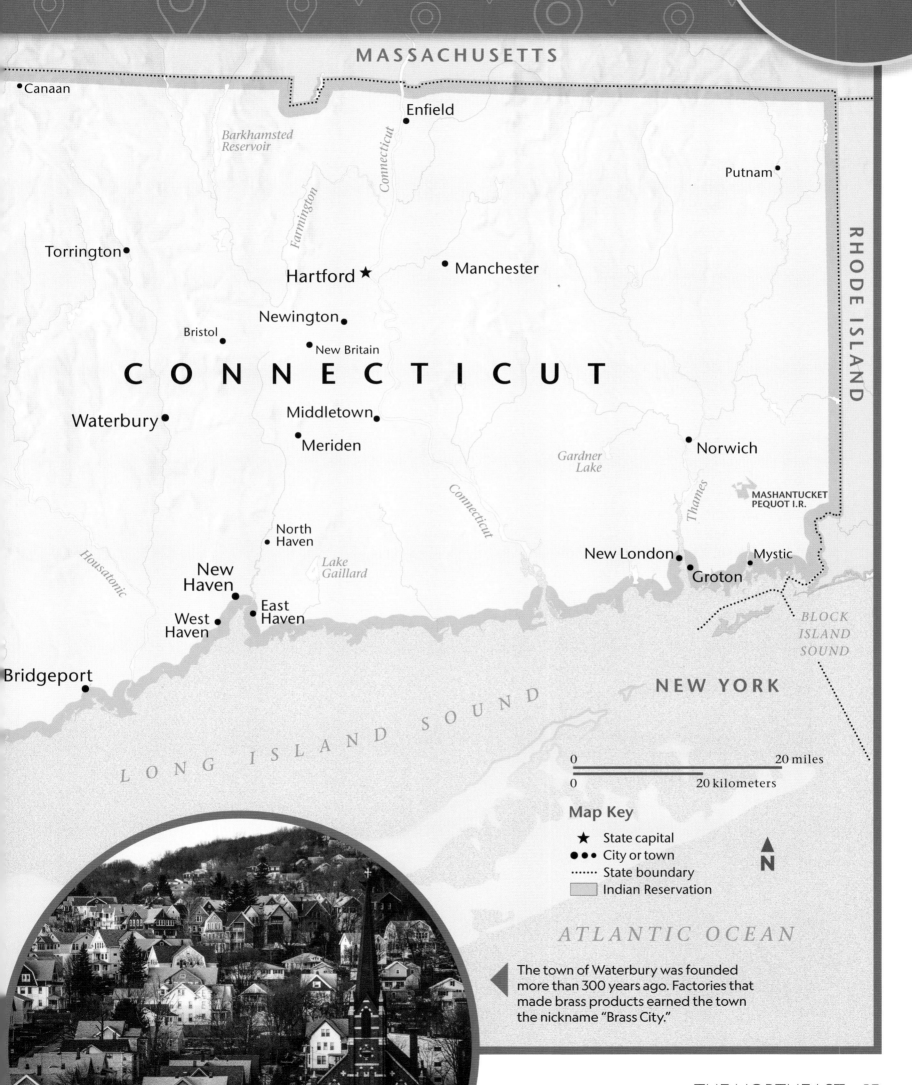

MASSACHUSETTS

•Canaan

Enfield•

Barkhamsted Reservoir

Putnam•

Farmington

Connecticut

Torrington•

Hartford ★   •Manchester

Newington•

Bristol•

New Britain•

CONNECTICUT

RHODE ISLAND

Waterbury•

Middletown•

•Meriden

Gardner Lake

Norwich•

Connecticut

Thames

MASHANTUCKET PEQUOT I.R.

North •Haven

Lake Gaillard

New London•   Mystic•

Housatonic

New Haven

Groton•

East Haven•

BLOCK ISLAND SOUND

West Haven•

Bridgeport•

NEW YORK

LONG ISLAND SOUND

```
0                    20 miles
0            20 kilometers
```

Map Key

★   State capital
•••   City or town
·······   State boundary
▭   Indian Reservation

N

ATLANTIC OCEAN

The town of Waterbury was founded more than 300 years ago. Factories that made brass products earned the town the nickname "Brass City."

DELAWARE

LAND & WATER
The Barrier Islands, Cypress Swamp, and Delaware Bay are important land and water features of Delaware.

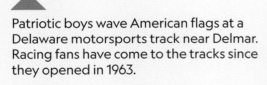

STATEHOOD
Delaware became the 1st state in 1787.

PEOPLE & PLACES
The population of Delaware is 967,171. Dover is the state capital. The largest city is Wilmington.

FUN FACT
Each year contestants bring pumpkins and launching machines to the Punkin Chunkin World Championship in Bridgeville to see who can toss their big orange squash the farthest.

The Delmarva Peninsula is a major area for raising chickens, with more than 1,500 poultry farms. The Delmarva poultry trade association is in Georgetown.

Patriotic boys wave American flags at a Delaware motorsports track near Delmar. Racing fans have come to the tracks since they opened in 1963.

Delaware State Flag

DECEMBER 7, 1787

Brightly colored umbrellas dot Cape Henlopen Beach. Sun, sand, and surf attract thousands of vacationers each year to Delaware's shore.

Peach Blossom
State Flower

Blue Hen Chicken
State Bird

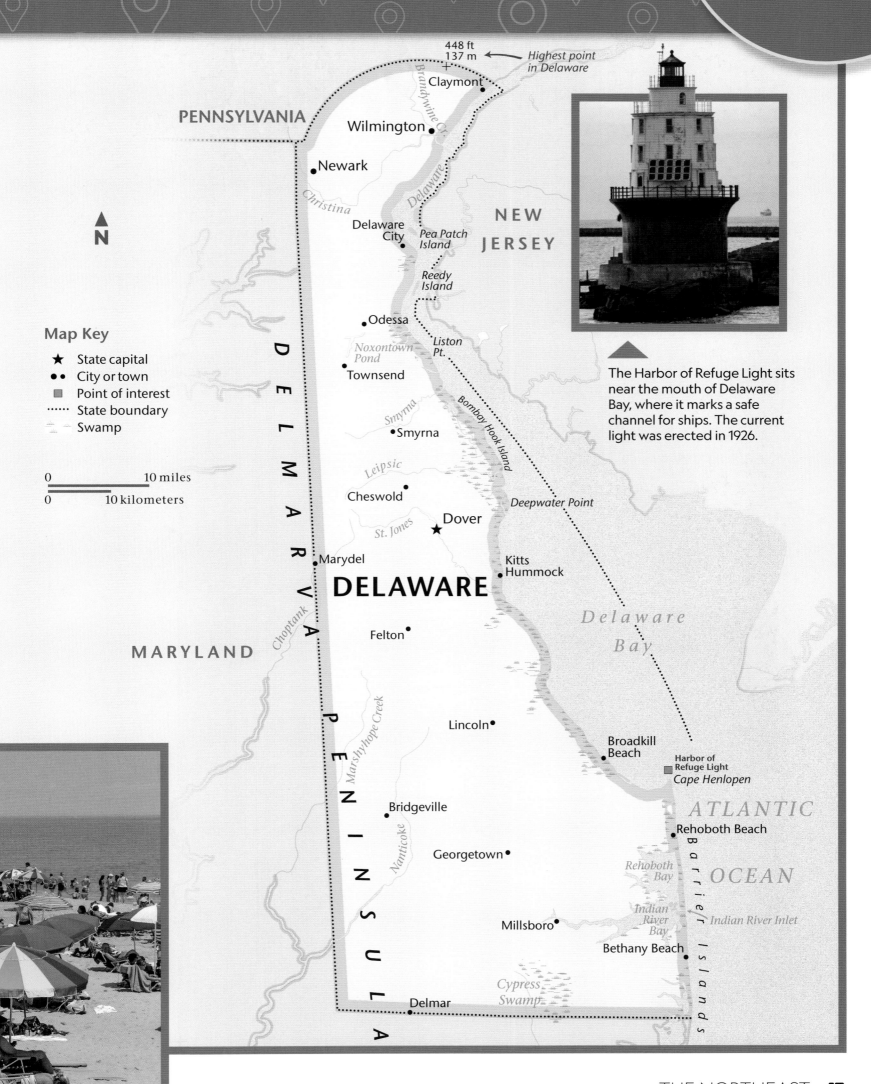

PENNSYLVANIA

NEW JERSEY

MARYLAND

DELAWARE

DELAWARE PENINSULA

448 ft
137 m ← Highest point
in Delaware

Claymont

Wilmington

Newark

Delaware City

Pea Patch Island

Reedy Island

Odessa

Liston Pt.

Noxontown Pond

Townsend

Smyrna

Bombay Hook Island

Leipsic

Cheswold

Deepwater Point

Dover

St. Jones

Marydel

Kitts Hummock

Delaware Bay

Felton

Marshyhope Creek

Choptank

Lincoln

Broadkill Beach

Harbor of Refuge Light
Cape Henlopen

Bridgeville

Nanticoke

Georgetown

ATLANTIC

Rehoboth Beach

Rehoboth Bay

OCEAN

Indian River Bay

Barrier Islands

Indian River Inlet

Millsboro

Bethany Beach

Cypress Swamp

Delmar

Christina

Brandywine Cr.

Delaware

Smyrna

Map Key
★ State capital
•• City or town
■ Point of interest
····· State boundary
🌿 Swamp

0 ——————— 10 miles
0 ——————— 10 kilometers

The Harbor of Refuge Light sits near the mouth of Delaware Bay, where it marks a safe channel for ships. The current light was erected in 1926.

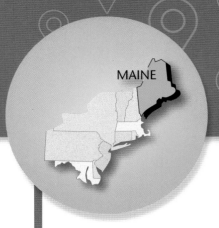

MAINE

 LAND & WATER The Appalachian Mountains, Mount Katahdin, and the Gulf of Maine are important land and water features of Maine.

 STATEHOOD Maine became the 23rd state in 1820.

 PEOPLE & PLACES Maine's population is 1,338,404. Augusta is the state capital. The largest city is Portland.

 FUN FACT During the last ice age, glaciers carved hundreds of bays and inlets along Maine's shoreline and created some 2,000 islands off the coast.

 There are 65 lighthouses along Maine's rocky coastline, warning ships of danger. The oldest lighthouse, Portland Head Light, is located at Cape Elizabeth.

Each year Rockland hosts the Maine Lobster Festival. This celebration of the state's popular seafood delicacy attracts visitors from far and near.

Maine State Flag

Moose are North America's largest deer, averaging six feet (2 m) tall at the shoulders. This female stands knee-deep in grass near Rangeley Lake.

White Pine Cone and Tassel
State Flower

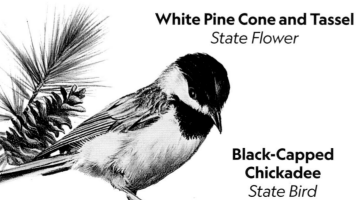

Black-Capped Chickadee
State Bird

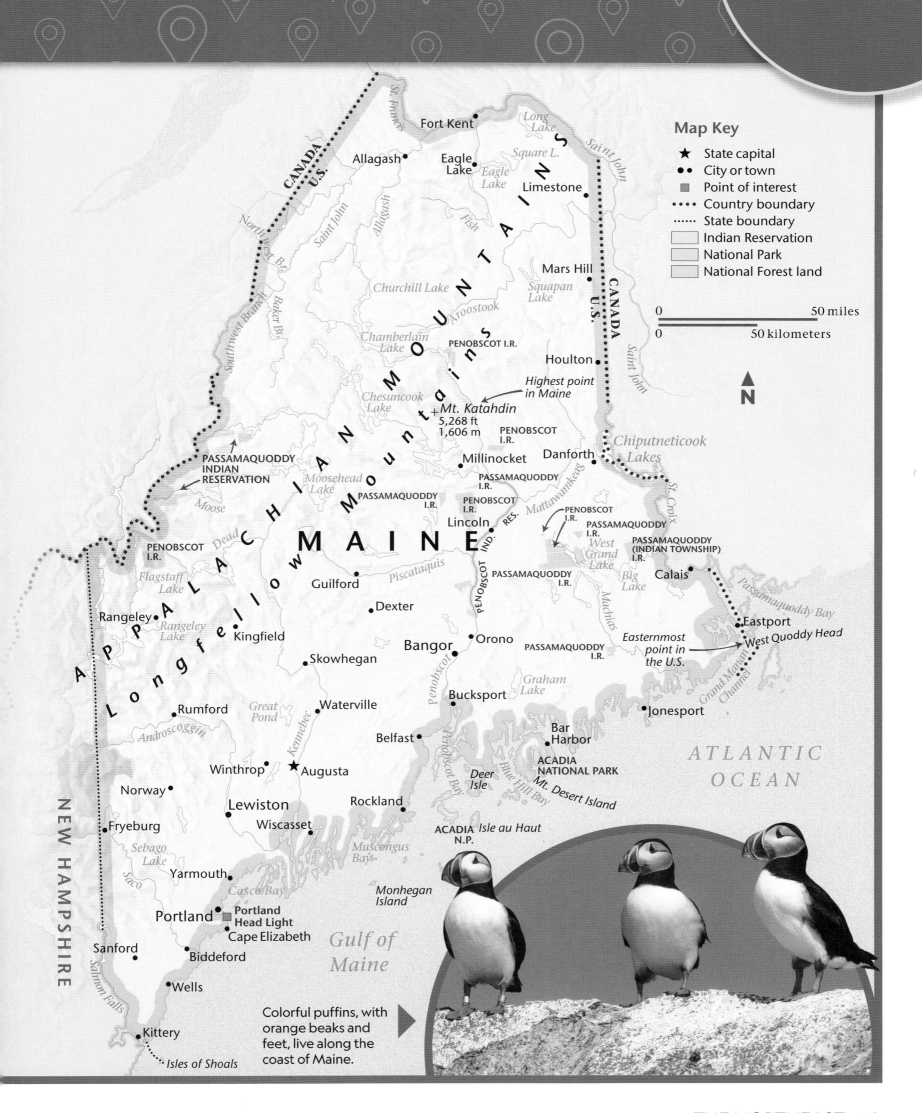

Fort Kent
Allagash
Eagle Lake
Limestone
Mars Hill

Long Lake
Square L.
Eagle Lake

CANADA
U.S.

Saint John
Northwest Br.
Southwest Branch
Baker Br.
Saint John
Allagash
Fish
Aroostook

Churchill Lake
Squapan Lake

CANADA
U.S.

Chamberlain Lake

PENOBSCOT I.R.

Houlton

Chesuncook Lake

Highest point in Maine
+ *Mt. Katahdin*
5,268 ft
1,606 m

PENOBSCOT I.R.

Danforth

Chiputneticook Lakes

Map Key
★ State capital
•• City or town
■ Point of interest
•••• Country boundary
···· State boundary
Indian Reservation
National Park
National Forest land

| 0 | | 50 miles |
| 0 | | 50 kilometers |

N

Millinocket

PASSAMAQUODDY I.R.

PENOBSCOT I.R.

Moosehead Lake

PASSAMAQUODDY I.R.

Lincoln

PENOBSCOT IND. RES.

Mattawamkeag

PENOBSCOT I.R.

West Grand Lake

PASSAMAQUODDY I.R.

PASSAMAQUODDY (INDIAN TOWNSHIP) I.R.

St. Croix

PASSAMAQUODDY INDIAN RESERVATION

Moose

PASSAMAQUODDY I.R.

Big Lake

Calais

Passamaquoddy Bay

PENOBSCOT I.R.

Flagstaff Lake

APPALACHIAN

Longfellow

Rangeley

Rangeley Lake

Kingfield

Dead

Guilford

Piscataquis

MAINE

Machias

Eastport

Grand Manan Channel

West Quoddy Head

Dexter

Easternmost point in the U.S.

Bangor
Orono

PASSAMAQUODDY I.R.

Rumford

Androscoggin

Skowhegan

Penobscot

Graham Lake

MOUNTAINS

Belfast

Bucksport

Jonesport

Great Pond

Waterville

Kennebec

Bar Harbor

ACADIA NATIONAL PARK
Mt. Desert Island

ATLANTIC OCEAN

Winthrop
★ Augusta

Norway

Rockland

Penobscot Bay

Deer Isle

Blue Hill Bay

ACADIA N.P.
Isle au Haut

Lewiston
Fryeburg
Wiscasset

Sebago Lake

Muscongus Bay

Monhegan Island

NEW HAMPSHIRE

Saco

Yarmouth

Casco Bay

Portland ■ **Portland Head Light**
Cape Elizabeth

Gulf of Maine

Sanford
Biddeford

Wells

Salmon Falls

Kittery

Isles of Shoals

Colorful puffins, with orange beaks and feet, live along the coast of Maine. ▶

MARYLAND

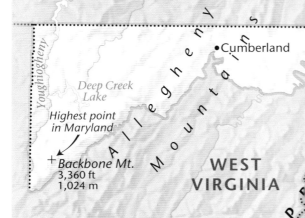

•Cumberland

Youghiogheny

Deep Creek Lake

Highest point in Maryland

$^+$*Backbone Mt.*
3,360 ft
1,024 m

Alleghe ny Mountains

WEST VIRGINIA

LAND & WATER The Appalachian Mountains, Potomac River, and Chesapeake Bay are major land and water features of Maryland.

STATEHOOD Maryland became the 7th state in 1788.

PEOPLE & PLACES Maryland's population is 6,042,718. Annapolis is the state capital. The largest city is Baltimore.

FUN FACT The name of Baltimore's professional football team—the Ravens—was inspired by a poem written by the famous American author Edgar Allan Poe, who lived in Baltimore in the mid-1800s.

Sailing is a popular pastime on Maryland's Chesapeake Bay. In the background, the Bay Bridge stretches 4.3 miles (6.9 km) across the waters of the bay.

Maryland State Flag

Since the early 1700s, Baltimore, near the upper Chesapeake Bay, has been a major seaport and a focus of trade, industry, and immigration.

Black-Eyed Susan
State Flower

Northern (Baltimore) Oriole
State Bird

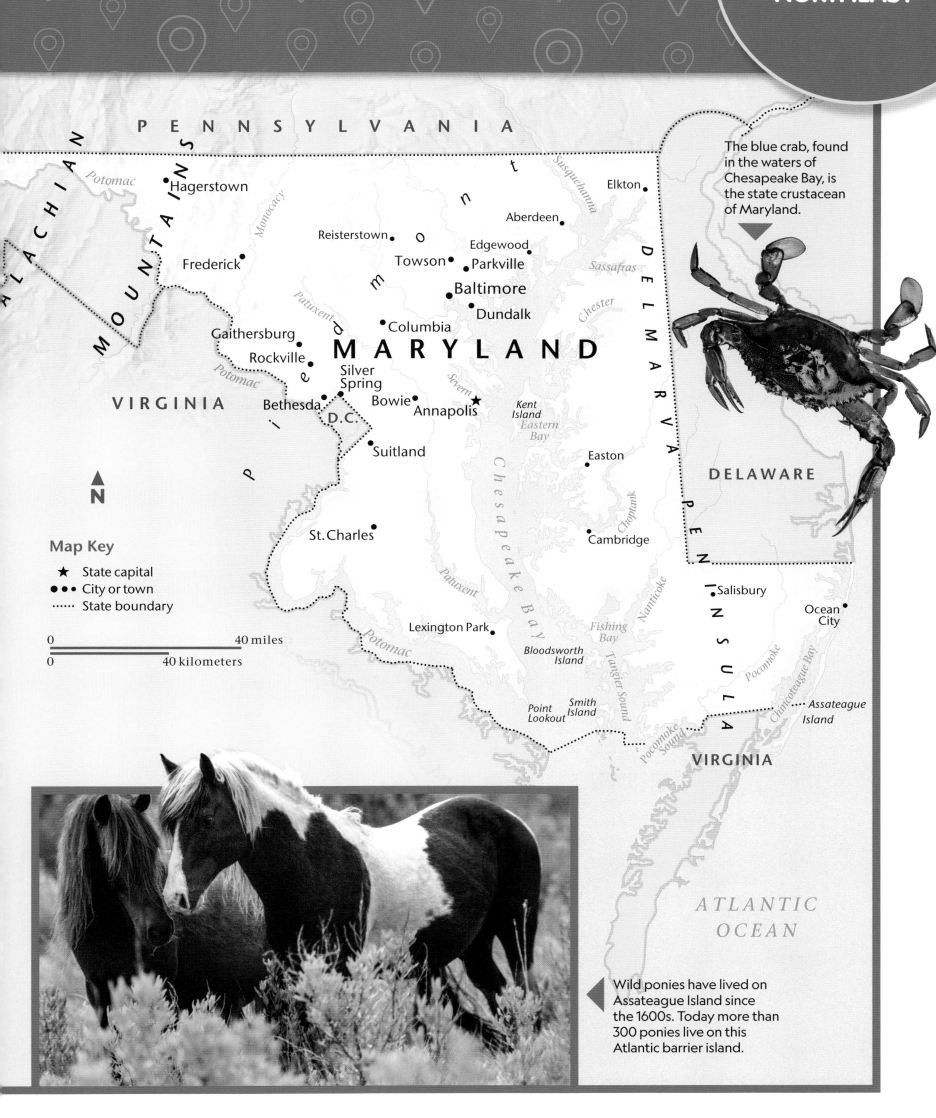

PENNSYLVANIA

Potomac

Hagerstown

Monocacy

Reisterstown

Frederick

Towson

Parkville

Baltimore

Dundalk

Columbia

MARYLAND

Gaithersburg

Rockville

Silver
Spring

Bowie

Bethesda

Annapolis

D.C.

Suitland

St. Charles

Lexington Park

Elkton

Aberdeen

Edgewood

Susquehanna

Sassafras

Chester

Kent
Island

Eastern
Bay

Severn

Easton

Chesapeake Bay

Choptank

Cambridge

Patuxent

Potomac

Potomac

APPALACHIAN

MOUNTAINS

VIRGINIA

Piedmont

Patuxent

DELMARVA PENINSULA

DELAWARE

Salisbury

Ocean
City

Nanticoke

Fishing
Bay

Bloodsworth
Island

Tangier Sound

Point
Lookout

Smith
Island

Pocomoke
Sound

Pocomoke

Chincoteague Bay

Assateague
Island

VIRGINIA

ATLANTIC
OCEAN

The blue crab, found in the waters of Chesapeake Bay, is the state crustacean of Maryland.

Map Key

★ State capital
•●• City or town
······ State boundary

0 ——————— 40 miles
0 ——————— 40 kilometers

N

Wild ponies have lived on Assateague Island since the 1600s. Today more than 300 ponies live on this Atlantic barrier island.

MASSACHUSETTS

MASSACHUSETTS

◀ The Green Monster, Fenway Park's famous left field wall, is 37 feet (11.3 m) high. The park is home to major league baseball's Boston Red Sox.

LAND & WATER The Berkshires, Cape Cod, and Nantucket Sound are important land and water features of Massachusetts.

STATEHOOD Massachusetts became the 6th state in 1788.

PEOPLE & PLACES The population of Massachusetts is 6,902,149. Boston is the state capital and the largest city.

FUN FACT In 1891 James Naismith wrote the original rule book for the game of basketball. Today the Basketball Hall of Fame is located in Springfield in his honor.

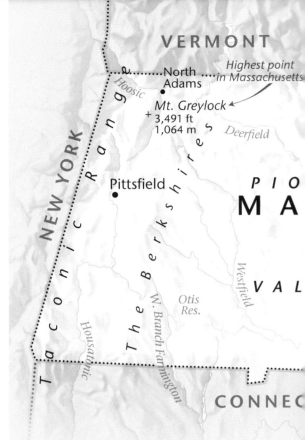

VERMONT

NEW YORK

Hoosic

North Adams

Highest point in Massachusetts

Mt. Greylock
+ 3,491 ft
1,064 m

Deerfield

Taconic Range

Pittsfield

The Berkshires

PIO

MA

Westfield

VAL

Otis Res.

W. Branch Farmington

Housatonic

CONNEC

Cranberries are a major agricultural crop in Massachusetts, which produces 24 percent of the cranberries grown in the United States. An annual cranberry harvest festival is held in Wareham.

▼

Massachusetts State Flag

Black-Capped Chickadee
State Bird

Mayflower
State Flower

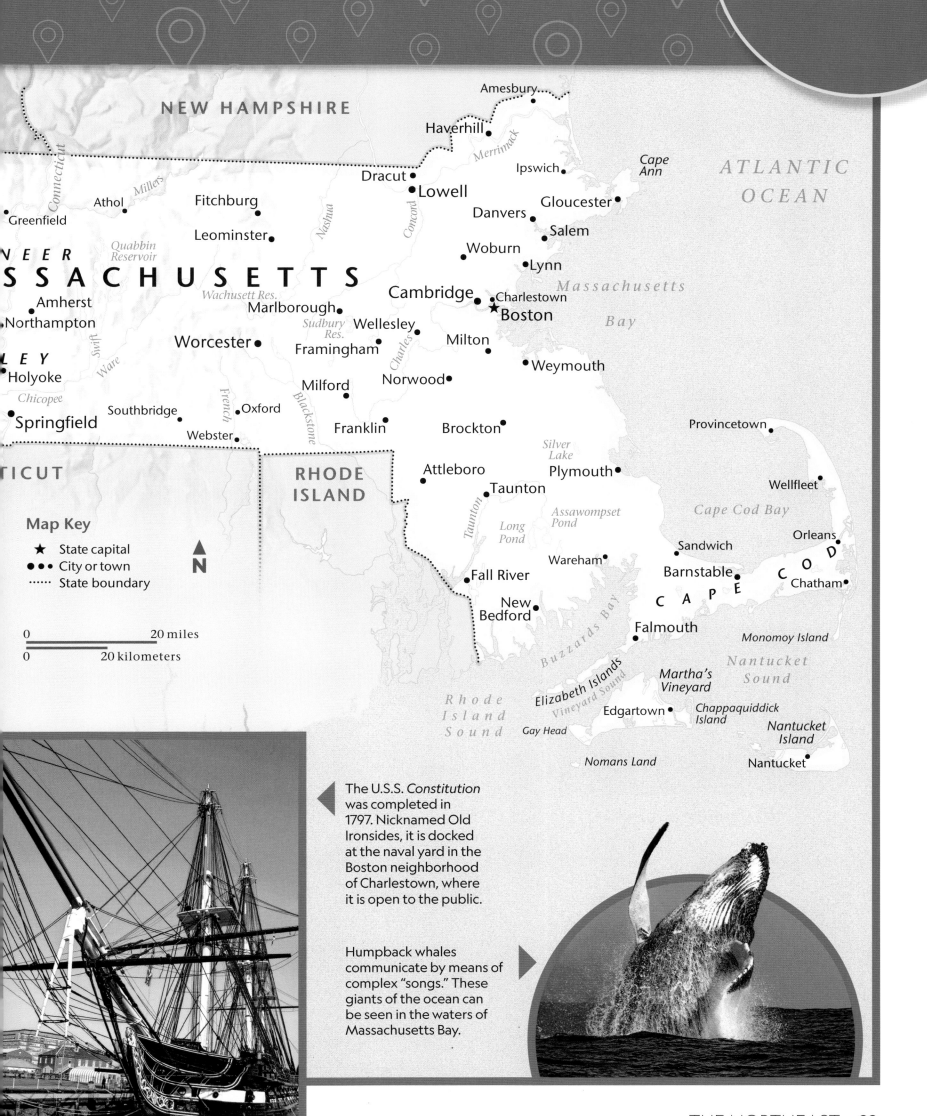

NEW HAMPSHIRE

ATLANTIC OCEAN

Connecticut

Athol
Millers
Fitchburg
Greenfield
Leominster

Amesbury
Haverhill
Dracut
Lowell
Merrimack
Ipswich
Cape Ann
Danvers
Gloucester
Woburn
Salem
Lynn

NEER
SSACHUSETTS
Quabbin Reservoir
Wachusett Res.
Marlborough
Cambridge
Charlestown
★ Boston
Massachusetts Bay

Amherst
Northampton
LEY
Holyoke
Swift
Ware
Chicopee
Nashua
Concord
Sudbury Res.
Wellesley
Framingham
Charles
Milton
Worcester
Weymouth
Norwood

Springfield
Southbridge
French
Oxford
Blackstone
Milford
Franklin
Webster

Brockton

Silver Lake

Provincetown

TICUT
RHODE ISLAND
Attleboro
Taunton
Taunton
Assawompset Pond
Plymouth
Wellfleet
Cape Cod Bay

Long Pond
Sandwich
Orleans

Map Key
★ State capital
●●● City or town
···· State boundary

N

0   20 miles
0   20 kilometers

Wareham
Barnstable
Chatham
C A P E   C O D

Fall River
New Bedford
Falmouth
Monomoy Island
Buzzards Bay
Nantucket Sound

Rhode Island Sound
Elizabeth Islands
Vineyard Sound
Martha's Vineyard
Edgartown
Chappaquiddick Island
Nantucket Island
Gay Head
Nomans Land
Nantucket

The U.S.S. *Constitution* was completed in 1797. Nicknamed Old Ironsides, it is docked at the naval yard in the Boston neighborhood of Charlestown, where it is open to the public.

Humpback whales communicate by means of complex "songs." These giants of the ocean can be seen in the waters of Massachusetts Bay.

NEW HAMPSHIRE

 LAND & WATER The White Mountains, Mount Washington, and the Merrimack River are important land and water features of New Hampshire.

 STATEHOOD New Hampshire became the 9th state in 1788.

 PEOPLE & PLACES New Hampshire's population is 1,356,458. Concord is the state capital. The largest city is Manchester.

 FUN FACT The first potato grown in the United States was planted in 1719 in Londonderry on the Common Field, now known simply as the Commons.

A golden dome topped by a war eagle rises above New Hampshire's State House in Concord. The pale granite building was completed in 1819.

Bitter cold and heavy snow are common in the White Mountains of New Hampshire, where snow tubing and skiing are popular winter sports.

New Hampshire State Flag

Mount Washington rises above trees rich with autumn colors. Soon winter will arrive, bringing the mountain some of the world's most extreme weather.

Purple Lilac
State Flower

Purple Finch
State Bird

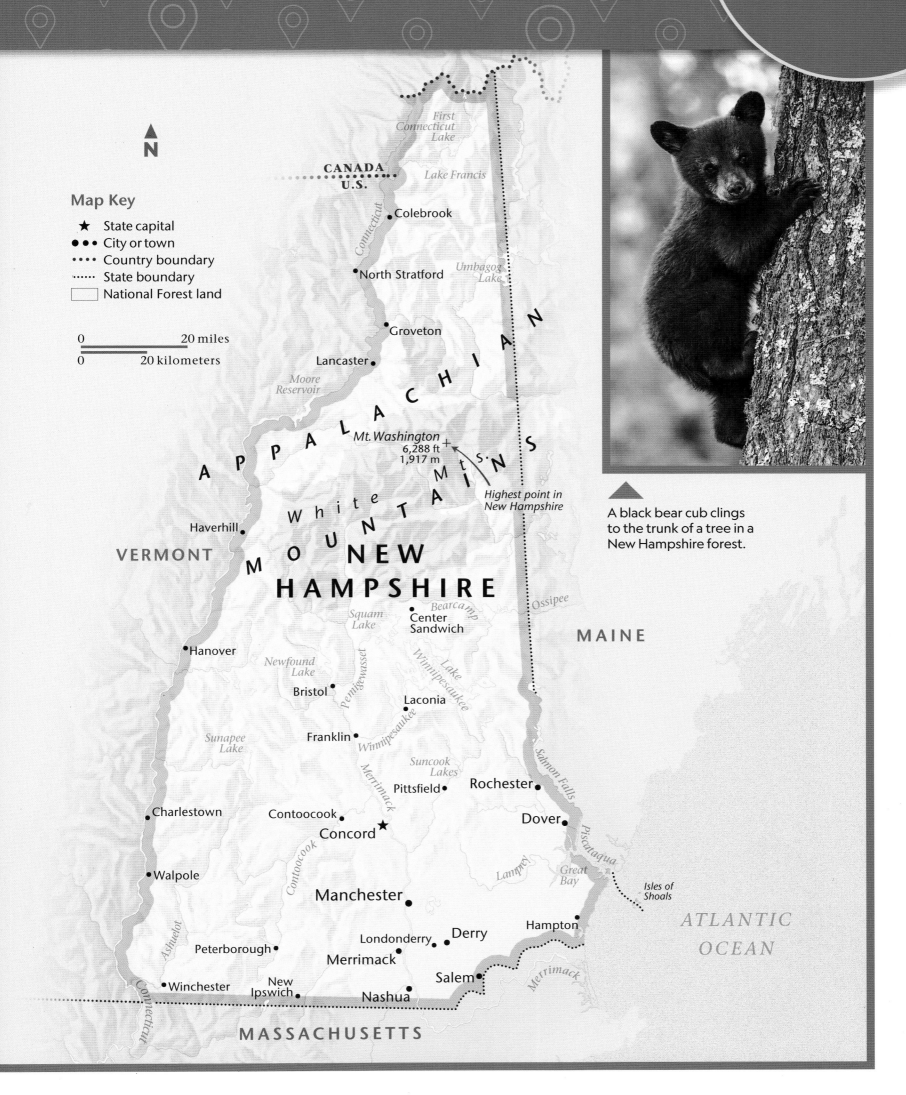

Map Key

★ State capital
• • • City or town
• • • • Country boundary
• • • • • State boundary
▭ National Forest land

0	20 miles
0	20 kilometers

CANADA
U.S.

First Connecticut Lake

Lake Francis

• Colebrook

Umbagog Lake

• North Stratford

Connecticut

• Groveton

Lancaster •

Moore Reservoir

APPALACHIAN

Mt. Washington
6,288 ft
1,917 m

Mts.

MOUNTAINS

Highest point in
New Hampshire

White

Haverhill •

VERMONT

MOUNTAINS

**NEW
HAMPSHIRE**

Squam Lake

Bearcamp

Center
Sandwich •

Hanover •

Newfound Lake

Pemigewasset

Lake Winnipesaukee

MAINE

Bristol •

Laconia •

Ossipee

Sunapee Lake

Franklin •

Winnipesaukee

Suncook Lakes

Merrimack

Pittsfield •

Rochester •

Salmon Falls

Charlestown •

Contoocook •

Concord ★

Dover •

Piscataqua

Contoocook

Walpole •

Ashuelot

Manchester •

Lamprey

Great Bay

Isles of Shoals

Peterborough •

Londonderry • Derry •

Hampton •

Merrimack •

New
Ipswich •

Salem •

Merrimack

**ATLANTIC
OCEAN**

Winchester •

Connecticut

Nashua •

MASSACHUSETTS

A black bear cub clings
to the trunk of a tree in a
New Hampshire forest.

NEW JERSEY

LAND & WATER
The Kittatinny Mountains, Cape May, and the Delaware River are important land and water features of New Jersey.

STATEHOOD New Jersey became the 3rd state in 1787.

PEOPLE & PLACES New Jersey's population is 8,908,520. Trenton is the state capital. The largest city is Newark.

FUN FACT The first dinosaur skeleton found in North America was excavated at Haddonfield in 1858. It was named *Hadrosaurus* in honor of its discovery site.

Sandy beaches on the Atlantic coast of New Jersey attract vacationers from near and far. Roller coasters are just one of the exciting rides in amusement parks along the shore.

New Jersey State Flag

Sunlight reflects off the skylines of Jersey City (foreground) and New York City (across the river). The second largest city in the state, Jersey City is home to many large corporations.

Street names, such as Kentucky Avenue and Tennessee Avenue, in the board game Monopoly are taken from actual street names in Atlantic City.

American Goldfinch
State Bird

Violet
State Flower

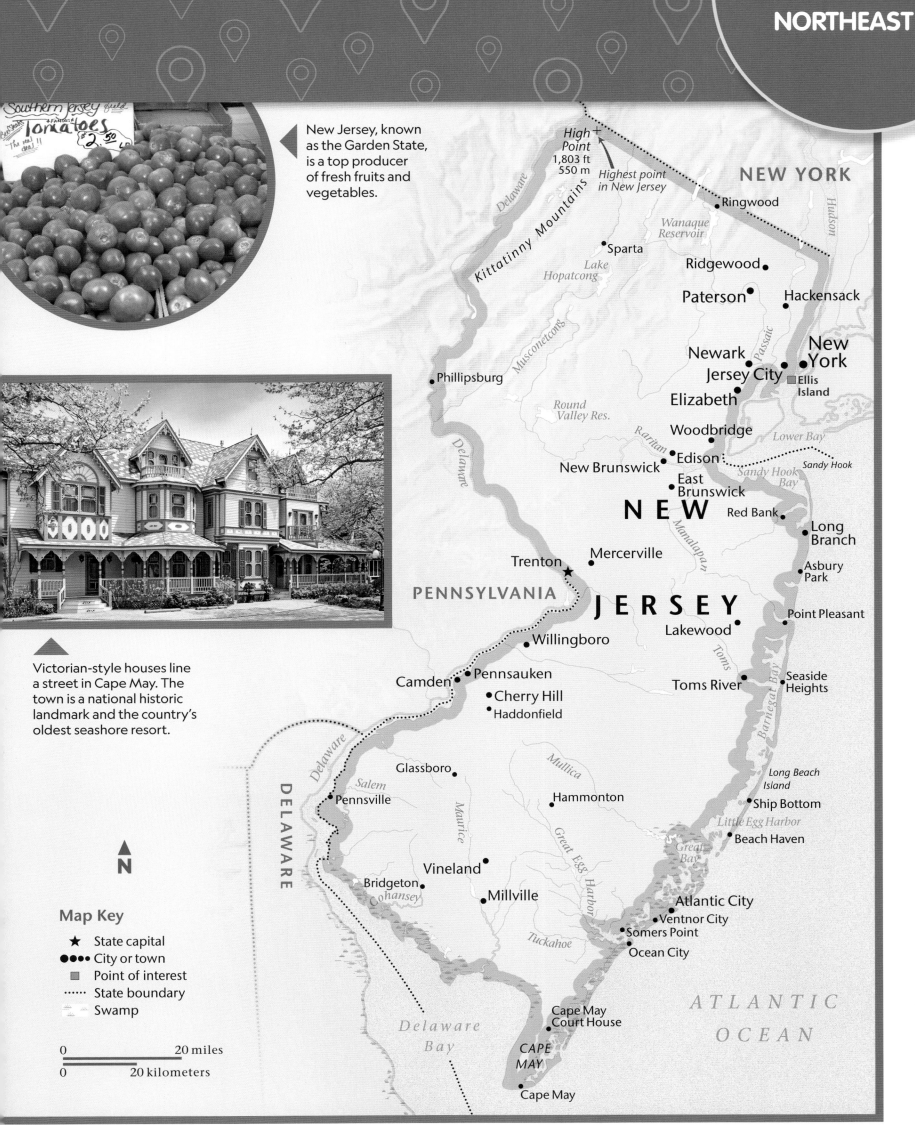

New Jersey, known as the Garden State, is a top producer of fresh fruits and vegetables.

Victorian-style houses line a street in Cape May. The town is a national historic landmark and the country's oldest seashore resort.

Map Key

★ State capital
●●● City or town
■ Point of interest
⋯ State boundary
〰 Swamp

0   20 miles
0   20 kilometers

N

NEW YORK

High Point
1,803 ft
550 m
Highest point in New Jersey

Ringwood

Delaware

Kittatinny Mountains

Sparta

Wanaque Reservoir

Ridgewood

Paterson   Hackensack

Lake Hopatcong

Musconetcong

Phillipsburg

Newark   **New York**

Jersey City

Passaic

Elizabeth   Ellis Island

Round Valley Res.

Woodbridge   *Lower Bay*

Raritan

Edison

New Brunswick   *Sandy Hook Bay*   *Sandy Hook*

East Brunswick

N E W   Red Bank

Manalapan   Long Branch

Trenton ★   Mercerville   Asbury Park

PENNSYLVANIA   **J E R S E Y**   Point Pleasant

Lakewood

Toms

Willingboro   *Barnegat Bay*

Camden   Pennsauken   Toms River   Seaside Heights

Cherry Hill

Haddonfield   *Long Beach Island*

Delaware   Glassboro   *Mullica*   Ship Bottom

Salem   *Little Egg Harbor*

Pennsville   Hammonton   Beach Haven

DELAWARE   *Maurice*   *Great Bay*

Great Egg Harbor

Bridgeton   Vineland

Cohansey   Millville   Atlantic City

Tuckahoe   Ventnor City

Somers Point

Ocean City

A T L A N T I C

Cape May
Court House   **O C E A N**

Delaware Bay   **CAPE MAY**

Cape May

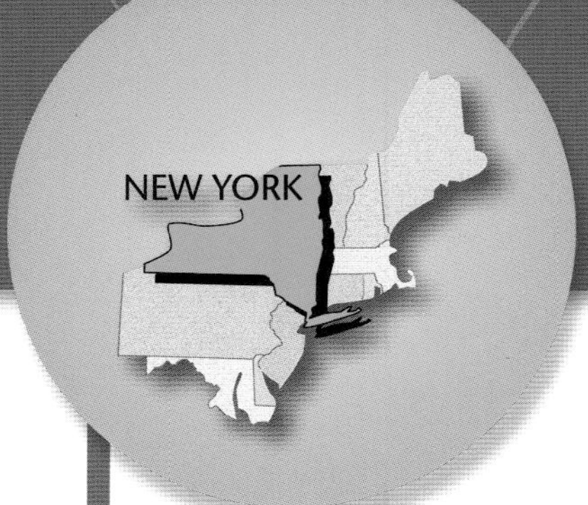
NEW YORK

NEW YORK

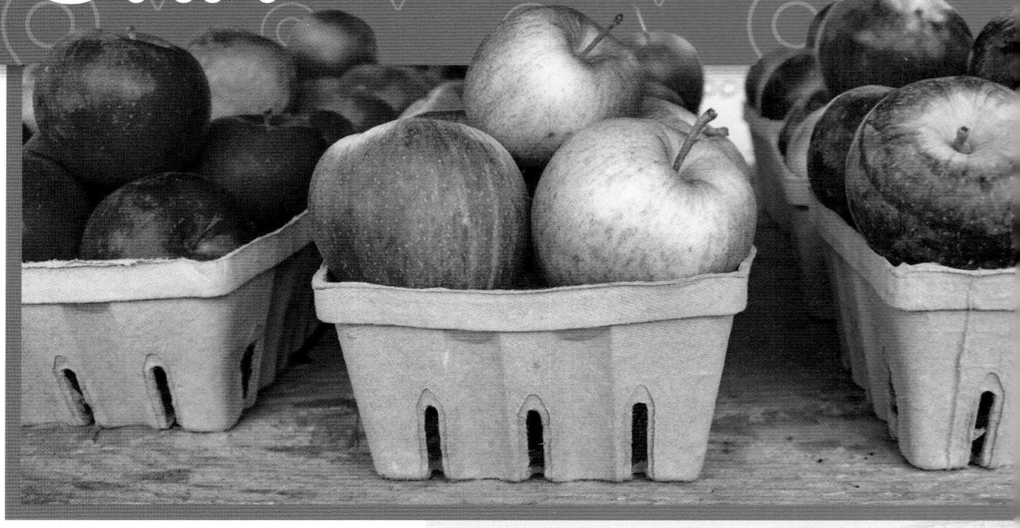

LAND & WATER

The Adirondack Mountains, the Finger Lakes, and the Hudson River are important land and water features of New York.

STATEHOOD New York became the 11th state in 1788.

PEOPLE & PLACES New York's population is 19,542,209. Albany is the state capital. The largest city is New York City.

FUN FACT The Erie Canal, built in the 1820s, connected Buffalo to the Hudson River at Albany, allowing ships to travel from the Atlantic Ocean to the Great Lakes. The canal contributed to the growth of New York City as a major trade center.

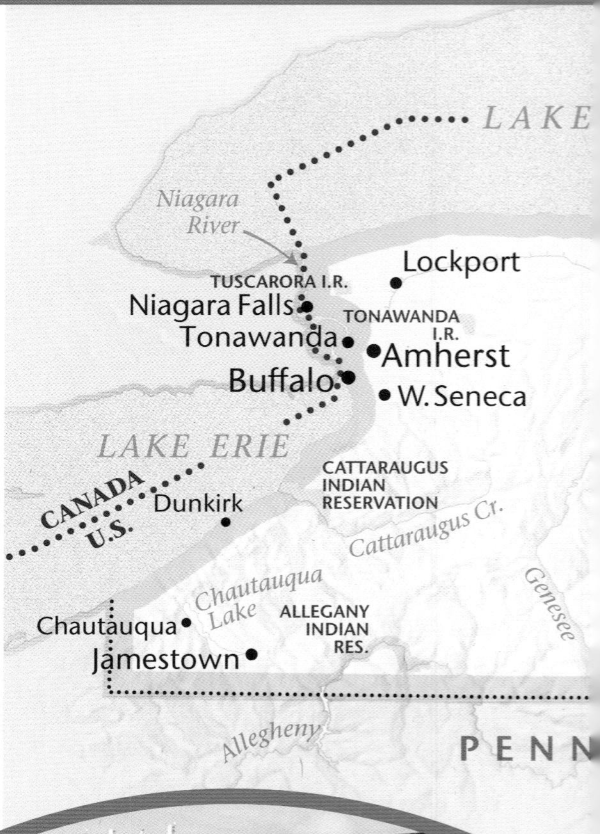
LAKE
Niagara River
Lockport
TUSCARORA I.R.
Niagara Falls
TONAWANDA I.R.
Tonawanda
Amherst
Buffalo
W. Seneca
LAKE ERIE
CANADA
U.S.
Dunkirk
CATTARAUGUS INDIAN RESERVATION
Cattaraugus Cr.
Genesee
Chautauqua Lake
Chautauqua
ALLEGANY INDIAN RES.
Jamestown
Allegheny
PENN

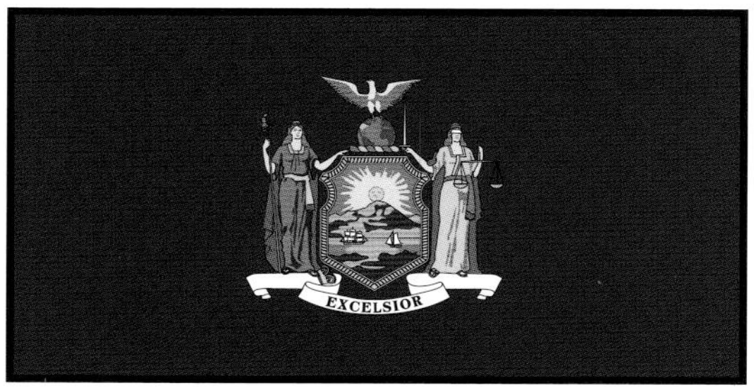
EXCELSIOR

New York State Flag

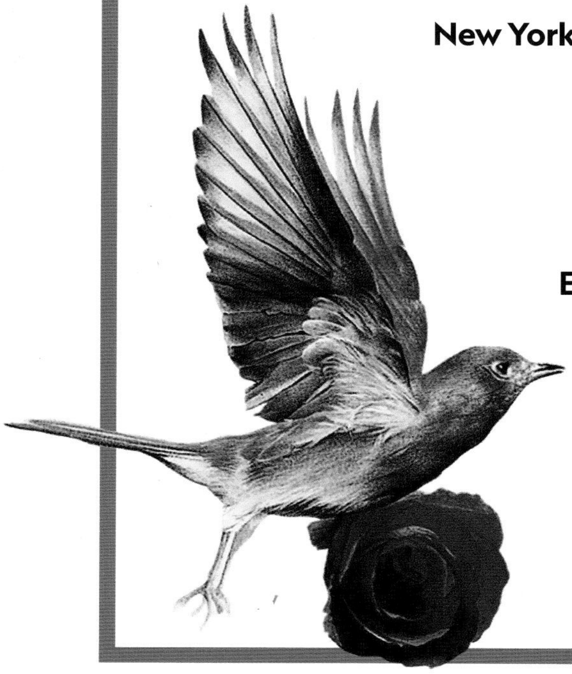

Eastern Bluebird
State Bird

Rose
State Flower

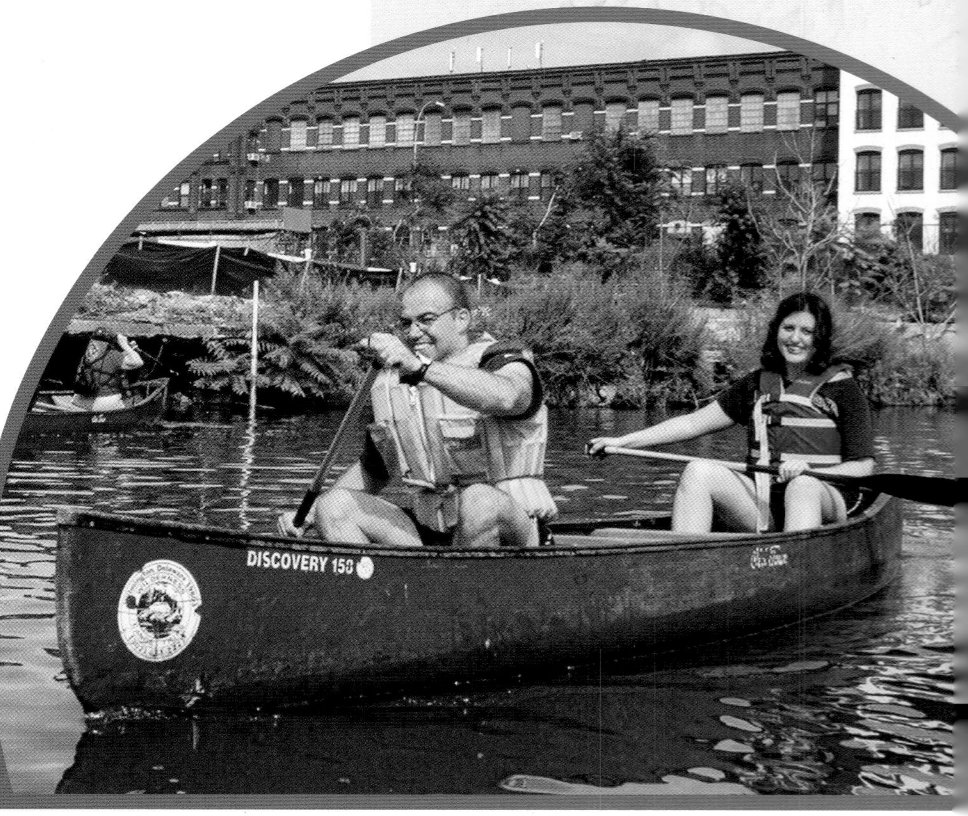
DISCOVERY 150

Fresh, juicy apples are on display at a roadside stand near Chautauqua. New York is the second largest producer of apples in the United States.

CANADA
ST. REGIS I.R. **U.S.**

Malone

Plattsburgh

Lake Champlain

Ogdensburg

St. Lawrence

Raquette

Lake Placid

A d i r o n d a c k

Thousand Islands

CANADA U.S.

Mt. Marcy +
5,344 ft
1,629 m

Highest point in New York

VERMONT

M o u n t a i n s *Lake George*

Watertown

Black

Hudson

ONTARIO

Oswego

Oswego

Oneida Lake

Rome

Glens Falls

Great Sacandaga Lake

Taconic Ranges

Greece

Erie Canal

Rochester

Utica

Saratoga Springs

A P P A L A C H I A N   M O U N T A I N S

Auburn

Syracuse
ONONDAGA
INDIAN RESERVATION

Mohawk

Schenectady

Seneca Lake

F i n g e r   L a k e s

Cayuga Lake

Cooperstown

Troy

Albany ★

MASSACHUSETTS

N E W   Y O R K

Keuka Lake

Ithaca

Hornell

Watkins Glen

Susquehanna

Catskill

Hudson

W. Br. Delaware

Elmira

Chemung

Binghamton

E. Branch

Catskill Mountains

Slide Mt.
+ 4,180 ft
1,274 m

Hudson

SYLVANIA

Susquehanna

Poughkeepsie

CONNECTICUT

Standing in New York Harbor, the Statue of Liberty, a gift from the people of France, is a symbol of freedom and democracy.

Delaware

Newburgh

Middletown

RHODE ISLAND

Block Island Sound

Long Island Sound

Montauk Point

Spring Valley

Yonkers

New Rochelle

Southampton

The Gowanus Canal, in the Brooklyn area of New York City, has been undergoing efforts to clean up its pollution. Here, people enjoy a canoe ride and the view from the water.

New York

Huntington

Brentwood

Gowanus Canal

New York Harbor

NEW JERSEY

Staten Island

Freeport

Long Beach

Long Island

ATLANTIC OCEAN

Map Key

★ State capital
●●●● City or town
◼ Point of interest
•••• Country boundary

— Erie Canal
···· State boundary
▢ Indian Reservation
▢ National Forest land

0   50 miles
0   50 kilometers

N ▲

PENNSYLVANIA

PENNSYLVANIA

 LAND & WATER The Allegheny Mountains, the Pocono Mountains, and the Susquehanna River are important land and water features of Pennsylvania.

 STATEHOOD Pennsylvania became the 2nd state in 1787.

 PEOPLE & PLACES Pennsylvania's population is 12,807,060. Harrisburg is the state capital. The largest city is Philadelphia.

 FUN FACT The town of Hershey is known as the Chocolate Capital of the World. The Hershey Company exports its chocolate candies to some 70 countries around the world.

Pennsylvania State Flag

Mountain Laurel
State Flower

Ruffed Grouse
State Bird

LAKE ERIE
• Erie
Corry •
Meadville • Titusville •
Pymatuning Reservoir
• Greenville
OHIO
• Sharon
Clarion •
Allegheny
Beaver
• New Castle
P
Kittanning •
Allegheny
Conemaugh
Ohio
• McCandless
Pittsburgh • • Penn Hills
• Washington
WEST VIRGINIA
Morrisville • • Uniontown
Monongahela
Cheat
Youghiogheny

Map Key
★ State capital
●●●● City or town
■ Point of interest
······ State boundary
----- Appalachian Trail
☐ National Forest land

0   25 miles
0   25 kilometers

N

◄ The Appalachian Trail stretches across more than 2,000 miles (3,200 km) from Maine to Georgia. The trail passes through 14 states, including Pennsylvania.

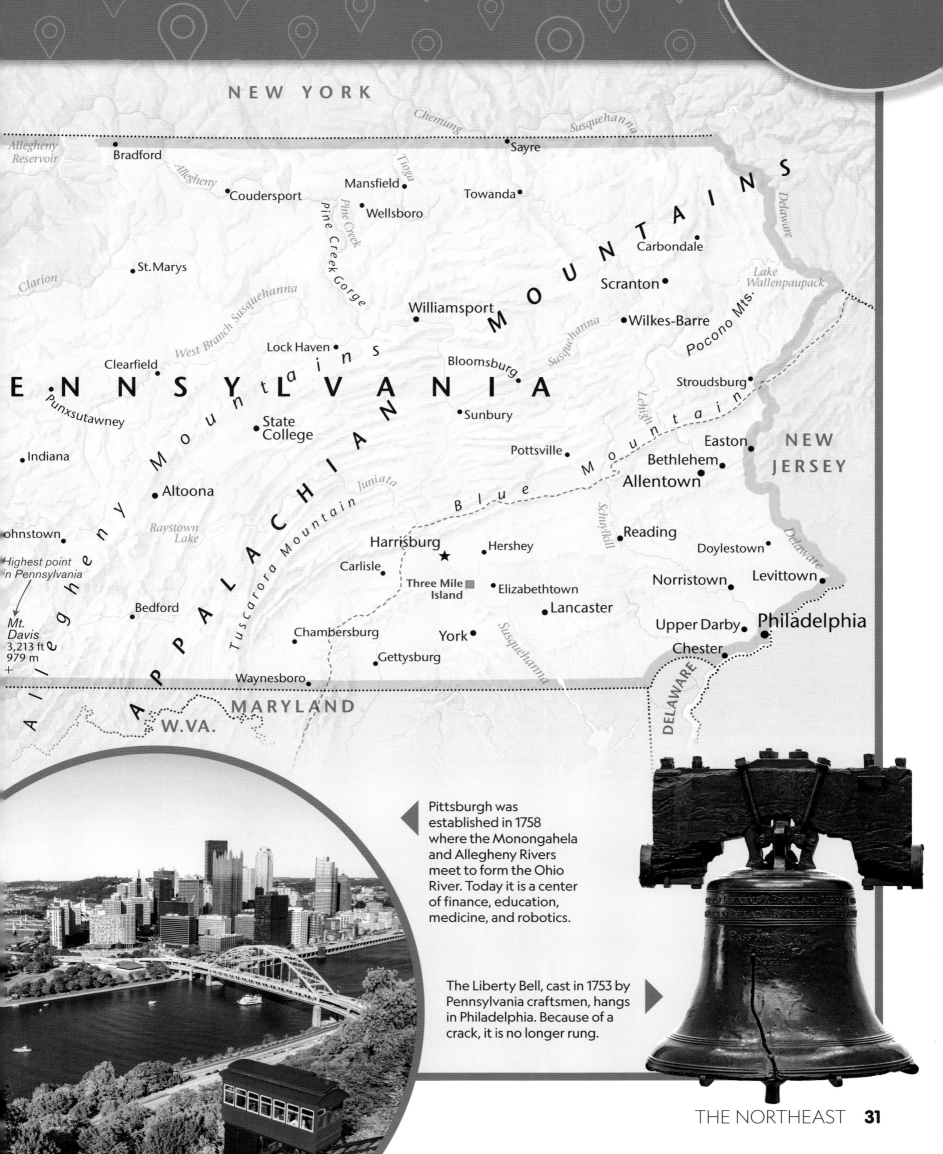

NEW YORK

Chemung
Susquehanna

*Allegheny
Reservoir*

Bradford

Allegheny

Coudersport

Mansfield

Tioga

Sayre

Towanda

Wellsboro

Pine Creek

Pine Creek Gorge

Carbondale

St. Marys

Scranton

*Lake
Wallenpaupack*

Clarion

West Branch Susquehanna

Williamsport

Wilkes-Barre

Pocono Mts.

M O U N T A I N S

Delaware

Lock Haven

Clearfield

Bloomsburg

Susquehanna

Stroudsburg

P E N N S Y L V A N I A

Lehigh

Punxsutawney

Mountains

Sunbury

State
College

Pottsville

Easton

Blue Mountain

Bethlehem

NEW
JERSEY

Indiana

Allentown

Altoona

Juniata

A P P A L A C H I A N

*Raystown
Lake*

Tuscarora Mountain

Schuylkill

Reading

Delaware

Johnstown

Allegheny

Doylestown

*Highest point
in Pennsylvania*

Harrisburg ★

Hershey

Norristown

Levittown

Carlisle

Bedford

Three Mile
Island

Elizabethtown

Upper Darby

Philadelphia

Mt.
Davis
3,213 ft
979 m
+

Chambersburg

Lancaster

York

Susquehanna

Chester

Gettysburg

DELAWARE

Waynesboro

M A R Y L A N D

W. VA.

Pittsburgh was
established in 1758
where the Monongahela
and Allegheny Rivers
meet to form the Ohio
River. Today it is a center
of finance, education,
medicine, and robotics.

The Liberty Bell, cast in 1753 by
Pennsylvania craftsmen, hangs
in Philadelphia. Because of a
crack, it is no longer rung.

RHODE ISLAND

 LAND & WATER Block Island and Narragansett Bay, with its many islands, are important land and water features of Rhode Island.

 STATEHOOD Rhode Island became the 13th state in 1790.

 PEOPLE & PLACES Rhode Island's population is 1,057,315. Providence is the state capital and the largest city.

? **FUN FACT** Rhode Island is the smallest U.S. state in size. It measures just 48 miles (77 km) from north to south and 37 miles (60 km) from east to west.

Sailing is a popular sport in Rhode Island. This boat is in full sail on a late summer day on Narragansett Bay.

Rhode Island State Flag

The North Lighthouse on the northern tip of Block Island still warns ships of dangerous waters. The building, constructed in 1867, does not have a typical lighthouse design.

Rhode Island has cold, snowy winters. Skaters enjoy ice-skating on City Center public rink in front of the historic city hall in Providence.

Violet
State Flower

Rhode Island Red
State Bird

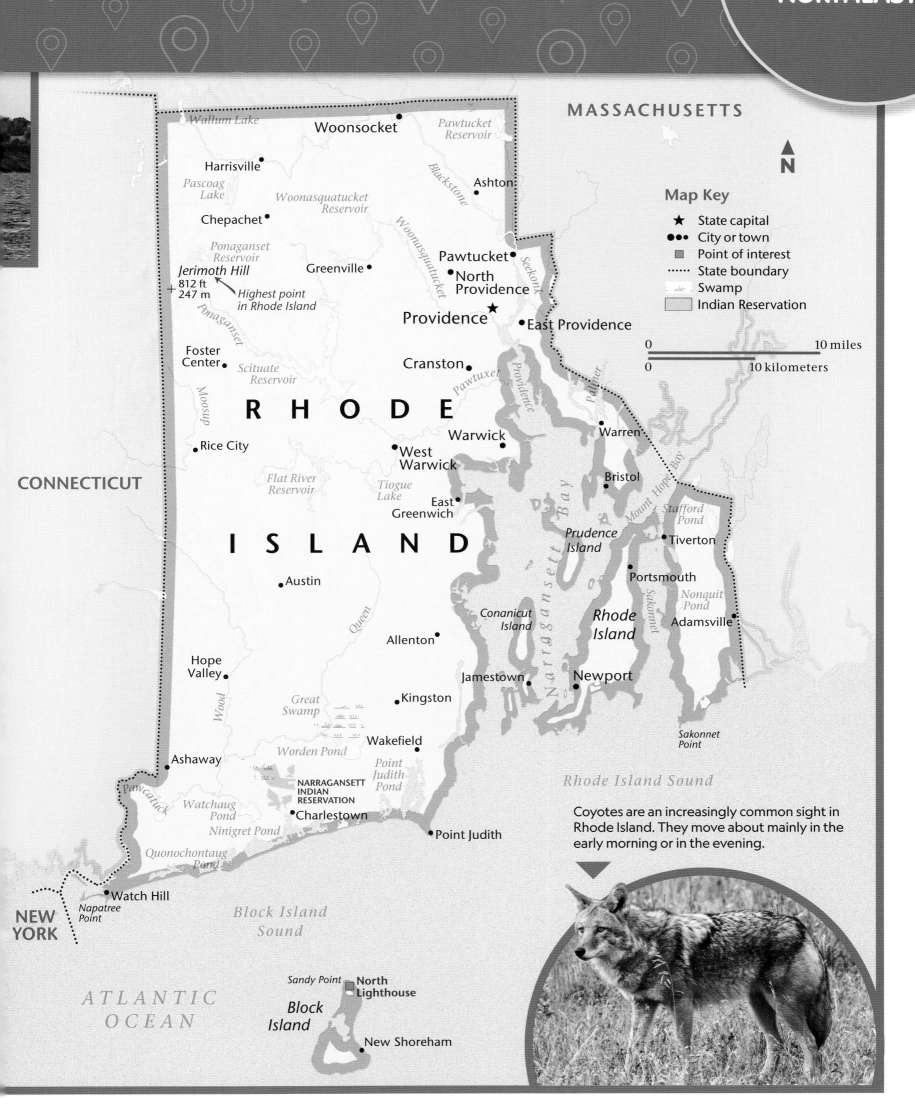

MASSACHUSETTS

Wallum Lake
Woonsocket
Pawtucket
Reservoir
Harrisville
Ashton
Pascoag
Lake
Blackstone
Woonasquatucket
Reservoir
Chepachet
Woonasquatucket
Ponaganset
Reservoir
Pawtucket
Greenville
Jerimoth Hill
North
Providence
+ 812 ft
247 m
Highest point
in Rhode Island
Providence
Seekonk
Ponaganset
East Providence
Foster
Center
Scituate
Reservoir
Cranston
Pawtuxet
Providence

Map Key
★ State capital
●●● City or town
■ Point of interest
⋯⋯ State boundary
Swamp
Indian Reservation

0   10 miles
0   10 kilometers

Moosup
R H O D E
Warwick
Warren
Rice City
West
Warwick
Bristol
Palmer
CONNECTICUT
Flat River
Reservoir
Tiogue
Lake
East
Greenwich
Stafford
Pond
I S L A N D
Prudence
Island
Tiverton
Narragansett Bay
Austin
Conanicut
Island
Portsmouth
Nonquit
Pond
Rhode
Island
Adamsville
Allenton
Sakonnet
Queen
Hope
Valley
Jamestown
Newport
Kingston
Wood
Great
Swamp
Sakonnet
Point
Wakefield
Ashaway
Worden Pond
Point
Judith
Pond
Rhode Island Sound
Pawcatuck
Watchaug
Pond
NARRAGANSETT
INDIAN
RESERVATION
Charlestown
Ninigret Pond
Point Judith
Quonochontaug
Pond
Coyotes are an increasingly common sight in
Rhode Island. They move about mainly in the
early morning or in the evening.
Watch Hill
NEW
YORK
Napatree
Point
Block Island
Sound
ATLANTIC
OCEAN
Sandy Point
North
Lighthouse
Block
Island
New Shoreham

VERMONT

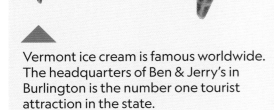

LAND & WATER The Green Mountains, Lake Champlain, and the Connecticut River are important land and water features of Vermont.

STATEHOOD Vermont became the 14th state in 1791.

PEOPLE & PLACES Vermont's population is 626,299. Montpelier is the state capital. The largest city is Burlington.

FUN FACT From the end of the Revolutionary War until 1791, Vermont was an independent republic with its own government and money. It even thought about uniting with Canada.

Vermont ice cream is famous worldwide. The headquarters of Ben & Jerry's in Burlington is the number one tourist attraction in the state.

People collect the sap of maple trees, which is boiled to make maple sugar and syrup. Maple production is celebrated each year at a festival in Tunbridge.

Vermont State Flag

Red Clover
State Flower

Hermit Thrush
State Bird

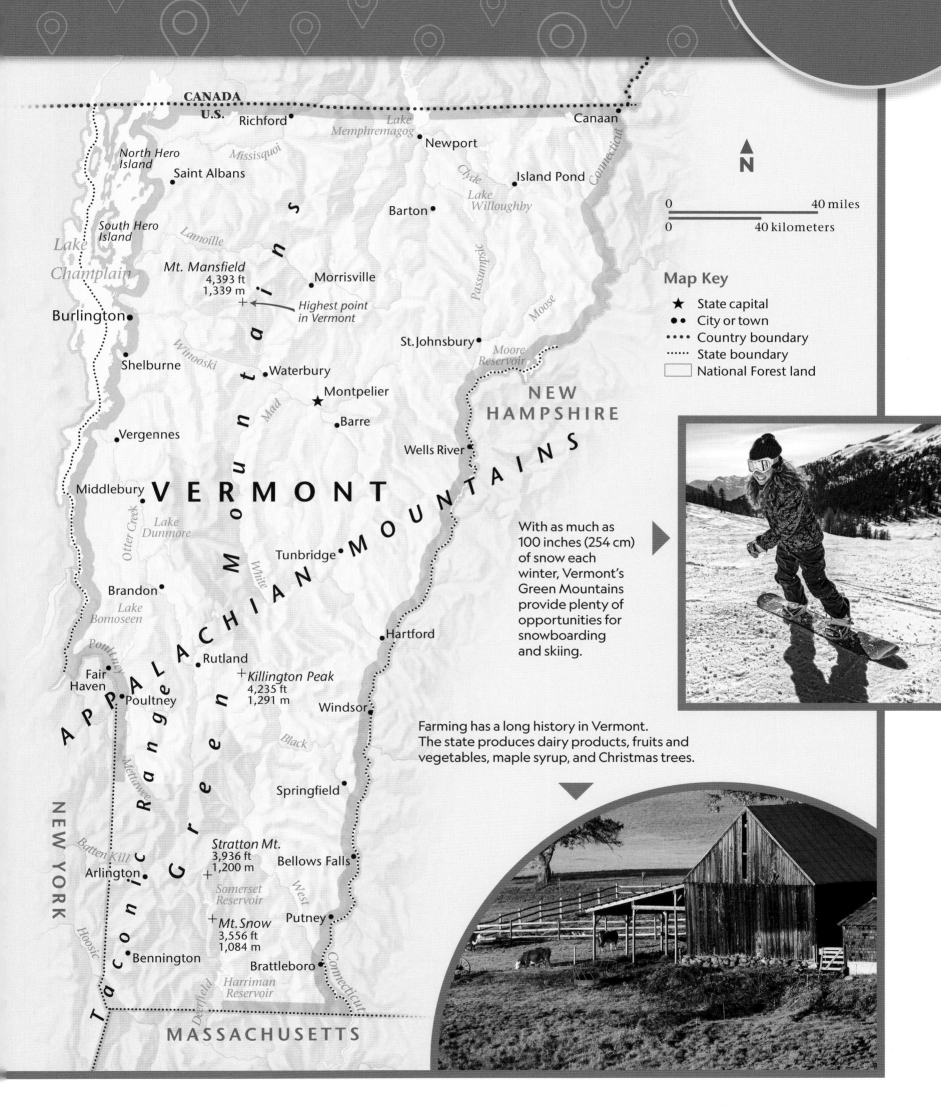

CANADA
U.S.

Richford

Lake Memphremagog

Newport

Canaan

North Hero Island

Missisquoi

Saint Albans

Clyde

Island Pond

Connecticut

Lake Willoughby

Barton

South Hero Island

Lamoille

Lake Champlain

Mt. Mansfield
4,393 ft
1,339 m

Morrisville

Passumpsic

Moose

Highest point in Vermont

Burlington

Winooski

Shelburne

Waterbury

St. Johnsbury

Moore Reservoir

Montpelier

**NEW
HAMPSHIRE**

Barre

Vergennes

Mad

Wells River

Middlebury

V E R M O N T

Otter Creek

Lake Dunmore

APPALACHIAN MOUNTAINS

Tunbridge

White

Brandon

Lake Bomoseen

Hartford

Poultney

Rutland

Fair Haven

Killington Peak
4,235 ft
1,291 m

Poultney

Windsor

Mettawee

Black

Springfield

**NEW
YORK**

Batten Kill

Arlington

Stratton Mt.
3,936 ft
1,200 m

Bellows Falls

Somerset Reservoir

West

Mt. Snow
3,556 ft
1,084 m

Putney

Hoosic

Bennington

Brattleboro

Deerfield

Harriman Reservoir

Connecticut

M A S S A C H U S E T T S

Appalachian
Taconic Range
Green Mountains

Map Key

★ State capital
●● City or town
••• Country boundary
···· State boundary
▭ National Forest land

0 ——————— 40 miles
0 ——————— 40 kilometers

With as much as 100 inches (254 cm) of snow each winter, Vermont's Green Mountains provide plenty of opportunities for snowboarding and skiing.

Farming has a long history in Vermont. The state produces dairy products, fruits and vegetables, maple syrup, and Christmas trees.

THE SOUTHEAST

T he Southeast is a region of varied landscapes. In the interior are old, worn-down mountains. Along the coasts there are wetlands and barrier islands. Cutting through these features are rivers that flow to the sea, linking the interior to distant places. The region's economic roots are in agriculture, especially cotton and tobacco, which were grown on large farms called plantations. Today the region is part of the Sunbelt, with rapidly growing cities and emerging high-tech industries.

Great egrets are a common sight in wetland areas of the coastal South. These young egrets in Florida stand in their treetop nest.

Live oak trees, some hundreds of years old, form a natural arch across a country road in Georgia. These trees, draped in Spanish moss, are common in the coastal Southeast.

ALABAMA

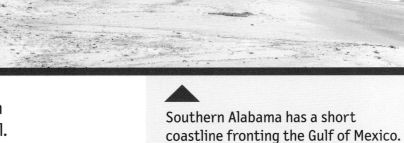

LAND & WATER The Appalachian Mountains, the Cumberland Plateau, and Mobile Bay are important land and water features of Alabama.

STATEHOOD Alabama became the 22nd state in 1819.

PEOPLE & PLACES Alabama's population is 4,887,871. Montgomery is the state capital. The largest city is Birmingham.

FUN FACT In Magnolia Springs, on Mobile Bay, mail is delivered by boat. The town has the country's only year-round, all-water mail route used by the U.S. Postal Service.

Southern Alabama has a short coastline fronting the Gulf of Mexico. The beach resort of Gulf Shores is a popular tourist destination.

A welder repairs a boat in Bayou La Batre on Alabama's Gulf Coast. The town is a center for shipbuilding and seafood processing.

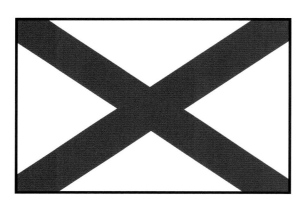

Alabama State Flag

This old railroad bridge, built in 1839, was a toll bridge across the Tennessee River. Today it is a pedestrian bridge.

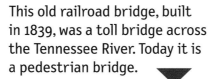

Northern Flicker
State Bird

Camellia
State Flower

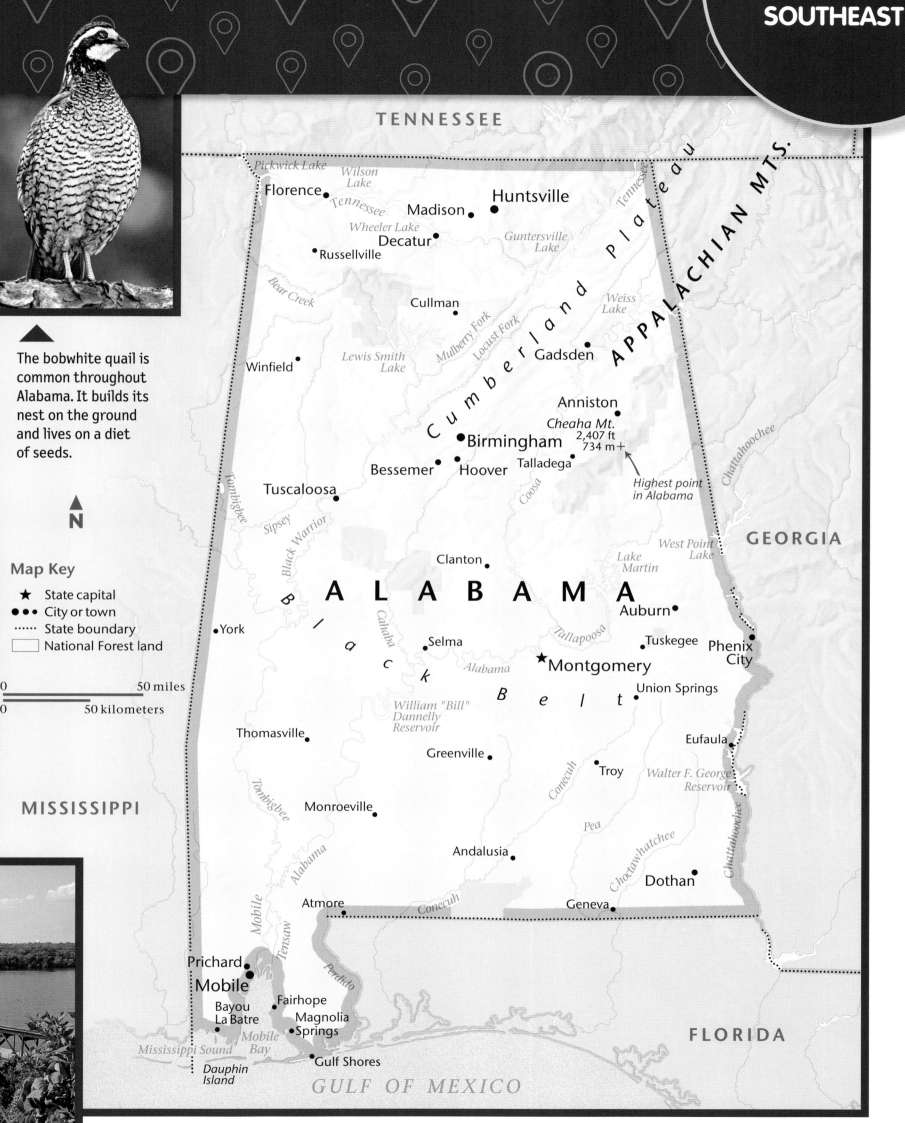

The bobwhite quail is common throughout Alabama. It builds its nest on the ground and lives on a diet of seeds.

N

Map Key
★ State capital
●●● City or town
...... State boundary
□ National Forest land

0 ————— 50 miles
0 ————— 50 kilometers

TENNESSEE

Pickwick Lake
Wilson Lake
Tennessee
Florence
Madison
Huntsville
Wheeler Lake
Decatur
Russellville
Guntersville Lake
Bear Creek
Cullman
Lewis Smith Lake
Mulberry Fork
Locust Fork
Weiss Lake
Gadsden
Winfield
Cumberland Plateau
APPALACHIAN MTS.
Tennessee
Anniston
Cheaha Mt.
2,407 ft
734 m +
Highest point in Alabama
Tombigbee
Birmingham
Bessemer Hoover Talladega
Coosa
Chattahoochee
Tuscaloosa
Sipsey
Black Warrior
GEORGIA
West Point Lake
Lake Martin
Clanton
A L A B A M A
Cahaba
York
Black
Selma
Alabama
★ Montgomery
Auburn
Tallapoosa
Tuskegee
Phenix City
Belt
Union Springs
William "Bill" Dannelly Reservoir
Eufaula
Thomasville
Greenville
Conecuh
Troy
Walter F. George Reservoir
MISSISSIPPI
Tombigbee
Monroeville
Pea
Andalusia
Choctawhatchee
Dothan
Alabama
Atmore
Conecuh
Geneva
Chattahoochee
Mobile
Tensaw
Perdido
Prichard
Mobile
Bayou La Batre
Fairhope
Magnolia Springs
Mobile Bay
FLORIDA
Mississippi Sound
Dauphin Island
Gulf Shores
GULF OF MEXICO

ARKANSAS

ARKANSAS

 LAND & WATER The Ouachita Mountains, the Ozark Plateau, and the Mississippi River are important land and water features of Arkansas.

 Arkansas became the 25th state in 1836.

 PEOPLE & PLACES Arkansas has a population of 3,013,825. Little Rock is the state capital and the largest city.

 FUN FACT In 1924 Crater of Diamonds State Park near Murfreesboro yielded the largest natural diamond ever found in the United States. The stone, called "Uncle Sam," weighed more than 40 carats.

Arkansas State Flag

Apple Blossom
State Flower

Mockingbird
State Bird

A farmer in eastern Arkansas checks the progress of his rice crop. The state is the leading U.S. producer of rice.

Located in the River Market District of Little Rock, the Museum of Discovery offers children interactive experiences in science, technology, engineering, and math.

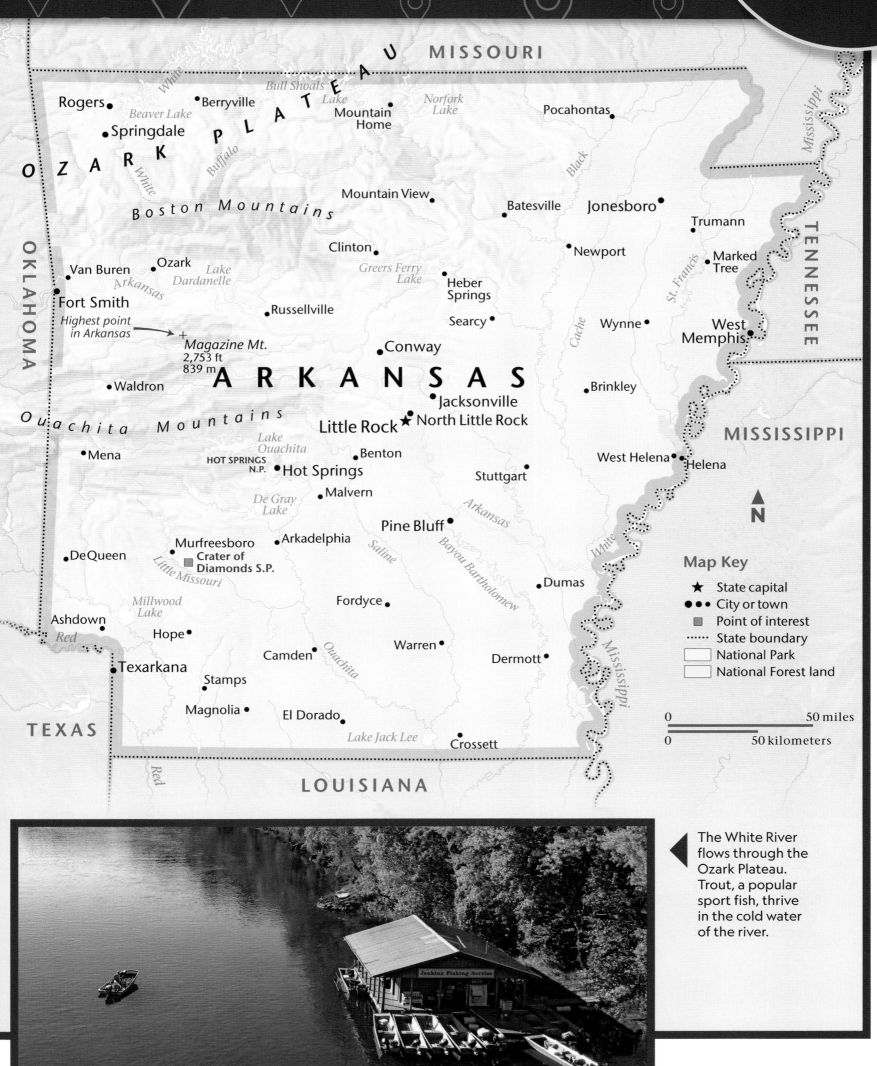

MISSOURI

OZARK PLATEAU

Rogers
Berryville
Beaver Lake
Springdale
White
Buffalo
Bull Shoals Lake
Mountain Home
Norfork Lake
Pocahontas

Boston Mountains

Mountain View
Batesville
Jonesboro
Trumann

White
Clinton
Greers Ferry Lake
Newport
Marked Tree

Van Buren
Ozark
Lake Dardanelle
Arkansas
Heber Springs

OKLAHOMA

Fort Smith
Russellville
Searcy
Black
St. Francis
Wynne
West Memphis

Highest point in Arkansas →
+ Magazine Mt. 2,753 ft 839 m

ARKANSAS

Conway

Cache

TENNESSEE

Waldron
Jacksonville
Brinkley

Ouachita Mountains
Little Rock ★ North Little Rock

MISSISSIPPI

Mena
Lake Ouachita
HOT SPRINGS N.P.
Benton
West Helena
Helena

Hot Springs
Stuttgart

De Gray Lake
Malvern
Arkansas

Pine Bluff
Bayou Bartholomew
White

DeQueen
Murfreesboro
Crater of Diamonds S.P.
Arkadelphia
Saline

Little Missouri

Fordyce
Dumas

N

Millwood Lake
Ashdown
Red
Hope
Warren
Dermott

Map Key
★ State capital
••• City or town
▪ Point of interest
···· State boundary
National Park
National Forest land

Texarkana
Stamps
Camden
Ouachita
Mississippi

TEXAS
Magnolia
El Dorado
Lake Jack Lee
Crossett

0 ——————— 50 miles
0 ——————— 50 kilometers

Red

LOUISIANA

◀ The White River flows through the Ozark Plateau. Trout, a popular sport fish, thrive in the cold water of the river.

FLORIDA

A L A B A

Britton Hill
345 ft
105 m

Highest point in Florida

Pensacola • Fort Walton Beach

 LAND & WATER The Florida Keys, the Everglades, and Lake Okeechobee are important land and water features of Florida.

 STATEHOOD Florida became the 27th state in 1845.

 PEOPLE & PLACES Florida's population is 21,299,325. Tallahassee is the state capital. The largest city is Jacksonville.

 FUN FACT Everglades National Park is home to rare and endangered species such as the American crocodile, the Florida panther, and the West Indian manatee.

The manatee is the state marine mammal of Florida. It averages 10 feet (3 m) in length and can weigh 1,000 pounds (450 kg).

NASA's powerful Space Launch System, shown in this artwork, is based at the Kennedy Space Center. It will support human exploration beyond Earth's orbit.

Florida State Flag

Orange Blossom
State Flower

Mockingbird
State Bird

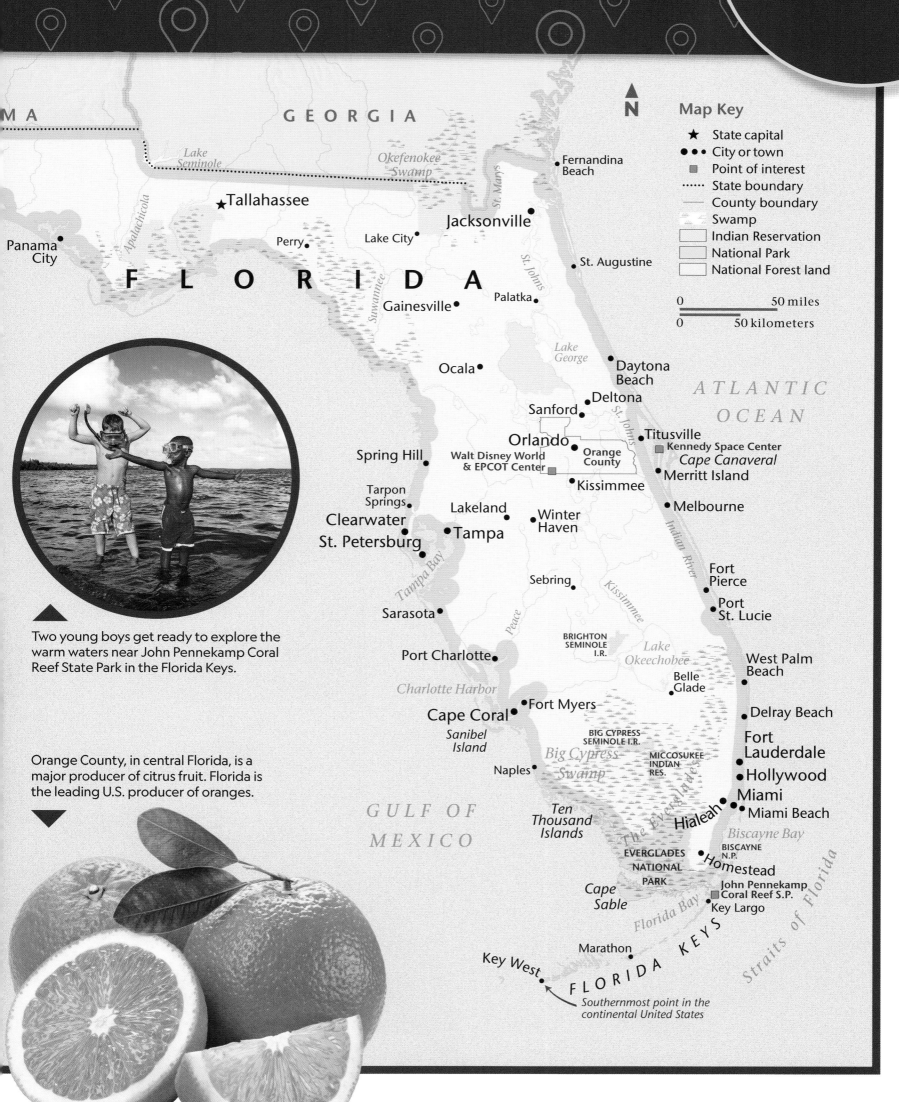

GEORGIA

★ Tallahassee

Panama City

F L O R I D A

Perry

Lake City

Jacksonville

Fernandina Beach

St. Augustine

Gainesville

Palatka

Ocala

Daytona Beach

Deltona

Sanford

Orlando

Titusville

Kennedy Space Center

Cape Canaveral

Merritt Island

Walt Disney World & EPCOT Center

Orange County

Kissimmee

Melbourne

Spring Hill

Tarpon Springs

Lakeland

Winter Haven

Clearwater

Tampa

St. Petersburg

Sebring

Fort Pierce

Port St. Lucie

Sarasota

Lake Okeechobee

BRIGHTON SEMINOLE I.R.

West Palm Beach

Belle Glade

Port Charlotte

Charlotte Harbor

Cape Coral

Fort Myers

Sanibel Island

BIG CYPRESS SEMINOLE I.R.

Big Cypress Swamp

MICCOSUKEE INDIAN RES.

Delray Beach

Fort Lauderdale

Hollywood

Naples

Miami

Miami Beach

Hialeah

Ten Thousand Islands

The Everglades

Biscayne Bay

BISCAYNE N.P.

EVERGLADES NATIONAL PARK

Homestead

Cape Sable

John Pennekamp Coral Reef S.P.

Key Largo

Florida Bay

Marathon

Key West

Southernmost point in the continental United States

F L O R I D A   K E Y S

Straits of Florida

GULF OF MEXICO

ATLANTIC OCEAN

Lake Seminole

Okefenokee Swamp

Apalachicola

Suwannee

St. Marys

St. Johns

Lake George

St. Johns

Indian River

Kissimmee

Peace

Tampa Bay

Map Key

★ State capital
••• City or town
■ Point of interest
······ State boundary
─── County boundary
Swamp
Indian Reservation
National Park
National Forest land

0 ——————— 50 miles
0 ——————— 50 kilometers

N

Two young boys get ready to explore the warm waters near John Pennekamp Coral Reef State Park in the Florida Keys.

Orange County, in central Florida, is a major producer of citrus fruit. Florida is the leading U.S. producer of oranges.

GEORGIA

GEORGIA

 LAND & WATER The Sea Islands, the Okefenokee Swamp, and the Savannah River are important land and water features of Georgia.

 STATEHOOD Georgia became the 4th state in 1788.

 PEOPLE & PLACES Georgia's population is 10,519,475. Atlanta is the state capital and the largest city.

 FUN FACT The Georgia Aquarium in Atlanta is the largest aquarium in the world. It features more than 100,000 animals living in more than eight million gallons (30.3 million L) of water.

▲
Built for the 1996 Olympic Games, Centennial Olympic Park in Atlanta is the site of festivals and community events that attract an estimated three million visitors each year.

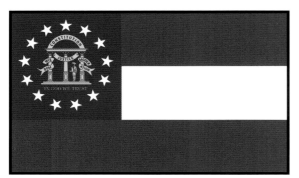

Georgia State Flag

Nearly half the peanut crop in the United States is grown in Georgia. Sylvester claims to be the peanut capital of the world. ▶

Alligators, which can live more than 50 years, are found in marshes, rivers, and swamps, including the Okefenokee National Wildlife Refuge.
▼

Cherokee Rose
State Flower

Brown Thrasher
State Bird

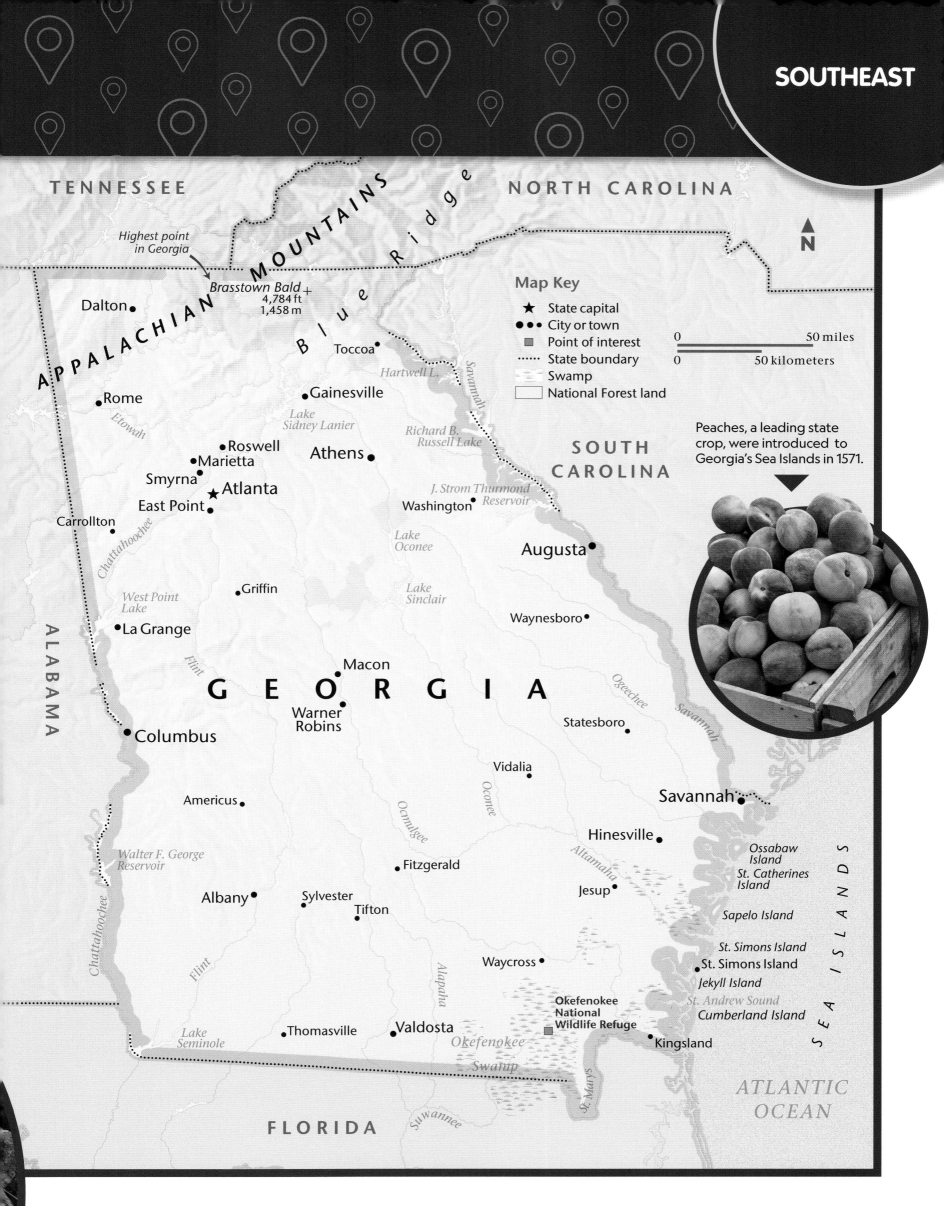

TENNESSEE

NORTH CAROLINA

APPALACHIAN MOUNTAINS

Blue Ridge

*Highest point
in Georgia*

Dalton •

Brasstown Bald +
4,784 ft
1,458 m

Rome •

Toccoa •

Hartwell L.

Gainesville •

Savannah

Map Key

★ State capital
••• City or town
■ Point of interest
•••• State boundary
   Swamp
   National Forest land

0 _____ 50 miles
0 _____ 50 kilometers

*Lake
Sidney Lanier*

*Richard B.
Russell Lake*

SOUTH
CAROLINA

Roswell •
Marietta •
Smyrna •
★ Atlanta
East Point •

Athens •

*J. Strom Thurmond
Reservoir*

Washington •

Peaches, a leading state
crop, were introduced to
Georgia's Sea Islands in 1571.

▼

Carrollton •

*Lake
Oconee*

Augusta •

Etowah

Chattahoochee

*West Point
Lake*

Griffin •

*Lake
Sinclair*

Waynesboro •

La Grange •

Flint

Macon •

G E O R G I A

Warner
Robins •

Ogeechee

Statesboro •

Savannah

Columbus •

ALABAMA

Vidalia •

Savannah •

Americus •

Ocmulgee

Hinesville •

Altamaha

*Ossabaw
Island*
*St. Catherines
Island*

*Walter F. George
Reservoir*

Albany •
Sylvester •

Oconee

Jesup •

Sapelo Island

SEA ISLANDS

Fitzgerald •

Tifton •

St. Simons Island
• St. Simons Island
Jekyll Island

Chattahoochee

Flint

Waycross •

Alapaha

Okefenokee
National
Wildlife Refuge ■

St. Andrew Sound
Cumberland Island

*Lake
Seminole*

Thomasville •

Valdosta •

*Okefenokee
Swamp*

Kingsland •

FLORIDA

Suwannee

St. Marys

ATLANTIC
OCEAN

KENTUCKY

KENTUCKY

Shaker Village in Pleasant Hill preserves the culture and history of the Shaker social movement.

 LAND & WATER Mammoth Cave, Lake Cumberland, and the Ohio River are important land and water features of Kentucky.

 STATEHOOD Kentucky became the 15th state in 1792.

 PEOPLE & PLACES Kentucky's population is 4,468,402. Frankfort is the state capital. The largest city is Louisville/Jefferson County.

 FUN FACT The song "Happy Birthday to You," one of the most popular songs in the English language, was written in 1893 by two sisters living in Louisville.

Abraham Lincoln, the 16th U.S. president, was born near Hodgenville. His profile appears on the penny.

ILLINOIS

Marion

Paducah
Calvert City
Kentucky Lake
Lake Barkley

MISSOURI

Mayfield

Fulton   Murray

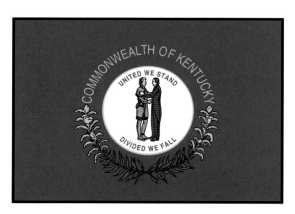

Kentucky State Flag

The setting sun turns the sky red over Cave Run Lake. The lake's natural beauty makes it a popular vacation spot.

Goldenrod
State Flower

Cardinal
State Bird

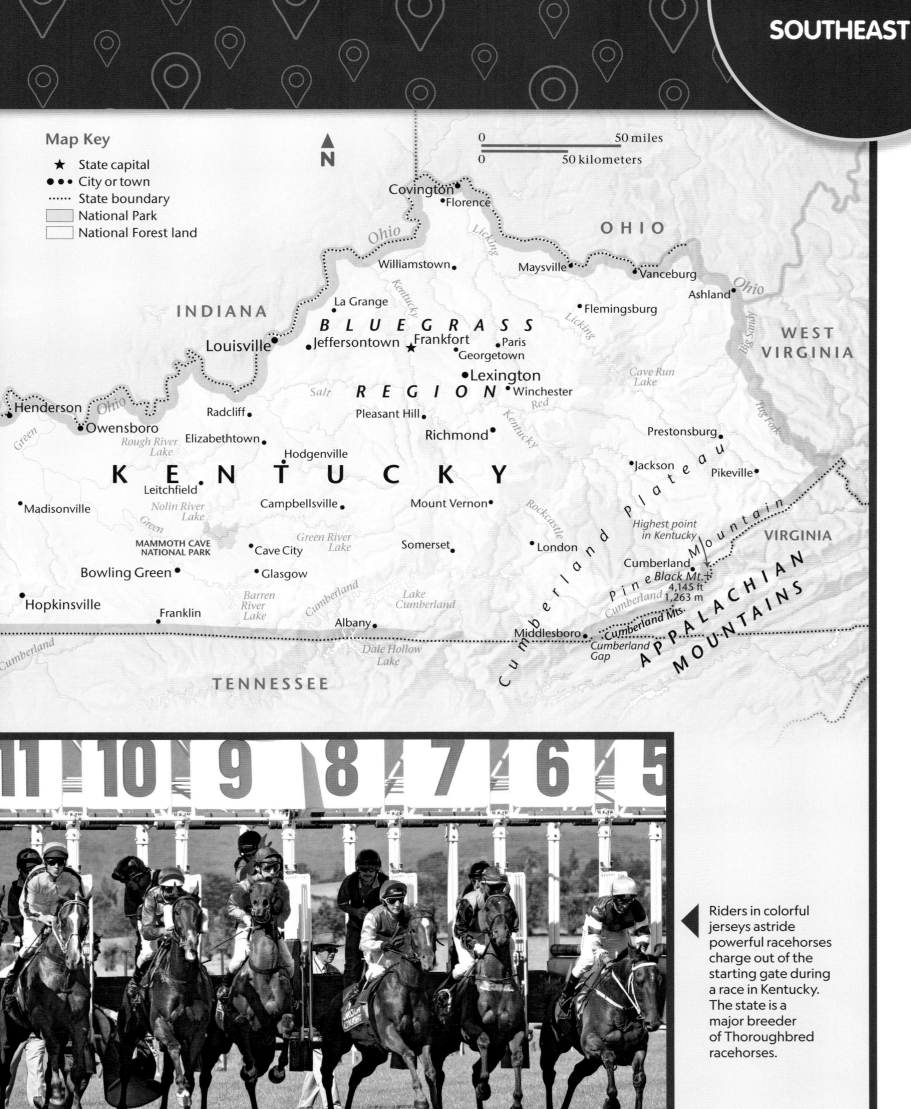

Map Key
★ State capital
••• City or town
······ State boundary
☐ National Park
☐ National Forest land

0 ————— 50 miles
0 ————— 50 kilometers

N

OHIO

Covington
Florence
Williamstown
Maysville
Vanceburg
Ashland
Flemingsburg

Ohio
Licking
Kentucky
Licking
Ohio
Big Sandy

INDIANA

La Grange

BLUEGRASS

WEST VIRGINIA

Louisville
Jeffersontown
★ Frankfort
Paris
Georgetown

REGION

Lexington
Winchester

Salt
Red

Cave Run Lake

Tug Fork

Henderson
Ohio
Radcliff
Pleasant Hill
Richmond
Kentucky
Prestonsburg

Green

Owensboro
Elizabethtown
Hodgenville
Jackson
Pikeville

Rough River Lake
Cumberland Plateau

K E N T U C K Y

Madisonville
Leitchfield
Campbellsville
Mount Vernon
Rockcastle
Highest point in Kentucky
VIRGINIA

Nolin River Lake
Green
Green River Lake
Somerset
London
Cumberland
Pine Mountain
Black Mt.
4,145 ft
1,263 m

MAMMOTH CAVE NATIONAL PARK
Cave City

Bowling Green
Glasgow
Barren River Lake
Cumberland
Lake Cumberland
Cumberland Mts.
APPALACHIAN MOUNTAINS

Hopkinsville
Franklin
Albany
Middlesboro
Cumberland Gap

Cumberland
Dale Hollow Lake

TENNESSEE

◄ Riders in colorful jerseys astride powerful racehorses charge out of the starting gate during a race in Kentucky. The state is a major breeder of Thoroughbred racehorses.

LOUISIANA

LAND & WATER Driskill Mountain, Lake Pontchartrain, and the Mississippi River are important land and water features of Louisiana.

STATEHOOD Louisiana became the 18th state in 1812.

PEOPLE & PLACES Louisiana's population is 4,659,978. Baton Rouge is the state capital. The largest city is New Orleans.

? **FUN FACT** The Louisiana state capitol building in Baton Rouge is the tallest of all the state capitols. It is a limestone skyscraper that stands 450 feet (137 m) tall and has 34 stories!

Louisiana State Flag

UNION JUSTICE CONFIDENCE

Magnolia
State Flower

Brown Pelican
State Bird

The steamboat *Natchez*, an authentic paddle-wheel boat, churns up water as it provides tourists with a view of New Orleans from the Mississippi River.

Louisiana is the leading U.S. producer of shrimp. Most of it is harvested from the Barataria-Terrebonne National Estuary of the Mississippi River.

Springhill

Red

Caddo Lake
■ Caddo Black Bayou Preserve

Bossier City

Shreveport

Lake Bistineau

• Mansfield

Red

Toledo Bend Reservoir

Natchitoches

• Many

Leesville •

TEXAS

De Ridder •

Sabine

Lake Charles •

Calcasieu Lake

Sabine Lake

Musicians practice on a park bench in New Orleans. The city is the birthplace of jazz, a music form that originated in African-American communities.

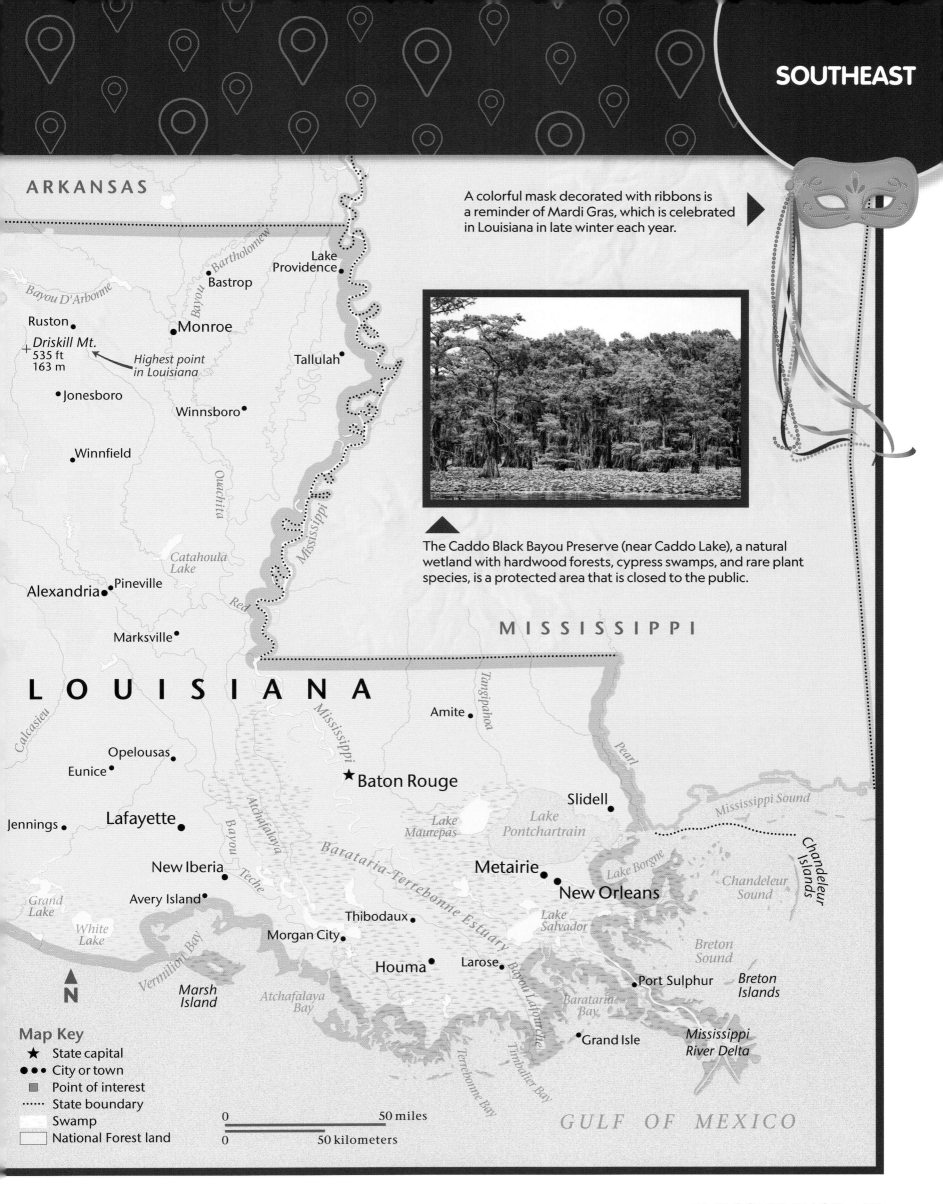

ARKANSAS

A colorful mask decorated with ribbons is a reminder of Mardi Gras, which is celebrated in Louisiana in late winter each year.

The Caddo Black Bayou Preserve (near Caddo Lake), a natural wetland with hardwood forests, cypress swamps, and rare plant species, is a protected area that is closed to the public.

Bayou D'Arbonne
Bayou Bartholomew
Lake Providence
Bastrop
Ruston
Monroe
+ Driskill Mt. 535 ft 163 m
Highest point in Louisiana
Tallulah
Jonesboro
Winnsboro
Ouachita
Winnfield

MISSISSIPPI

Catahoula Lake
Red
Alexandria Pineville
Marksville

LOUISIANA

Mississippi
Calcasieu
Amite
Tangipahoa
Opelousas
Eunice
★ Baton Rouge
Slidell
Pearl
Mississippi Sound
Lafayette
Jennings
Atchafalaya
Bayou
Lake Maurepas
Lake Pontchartrain
Lake Borgne
Chandeleur Islands
New Iberia
Teche
Barataria-Terrebonne Estuary
Metairie
New Orleans
Chandeleur Sound
Avery Island
Grand Lake
White Lake
Thibodaux
Lake Salvador
Breton Sound
Morgan City
Vermilion Bay
N
Marsh Island
Atchafalaya Bay
Houma
Larose
Bayou Lafourche
Barataria Bay
Port Sulphur
Breton Islands
Grand Isle
Mississippi River Delta
Terrebonne Bay
Timbalier Bay
GULF OF MEXICO

Map Key
★ State capital
••• City or town
■ Point of interest
···· State boundary
Swamp
National Forest land

0 50 miles
0 50 kilometers

MISSISSIPPI

LAND & WATER The Mississippi Petrified Forest, the Tennessee-Tombigbee Waterway, and the Mississippi River are important land and water features of Mississippi.

STATEHOOD Mississippi became the 20th state in 1817.

PEOPLE & PLACES The population of Mississippi is 2,986,530. Jackson is the state capital and the largest city.

FUN FACT Jim Henson, creator of Kermit the Frog, Miss Piggy, Big Bird, and other famous Muppets, was born in Greenville.

Mississippi is the leading producer of catfish in the United States. A part of the Mississippi River Valley known as the Delta is the main producing area.

Two bridges cross the Mississippi River between Vicksburg, Mississippi, and Delta, Louisiana. Cars and trucks use one bridge (left). The other is for trains.

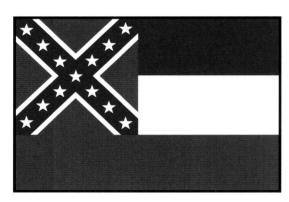

Mississippi State Flag

A sandy beach near Biloxi, on the state's Gulf of Mexico coast, is ready for sunseeking tourists.

Mockingbird
State Bird

Magnolia
State Flower

More than 800 cotton farms produce over 1.4 million bales (about 500 pounds/227 kg per bale) of cotton each year in Mississippi.

N

Map Key

★ State capital
•• City or town
■ Point of interest
···· State boundary
▨ Indian Reservation
☐ National Forest land

0 ——————— 50 miles
0 ——————— 50 kilometers

TENNESSEE

ARKANSAS

LOUISIANA

ALABAMA

Mississippi

Coldwater

Southaven
Corinth
Pickwick Lake

Senatobia
Booneville
Woodall Mt. +
806 ft
246 m

Sardis Lake
New Albany
Tennessee-Tombigbee Waterway

Little Tallahatchie
Oxford
Tupelo

Yocona

Clarksdale
Water Valley

Houston
Aberdeen

Yalobusha

Shelby

Ruleville
West Point

Tallahatchie

Tombigbee

D E L T A
Winona
Columbus

Indianola

Greenville

Yazoo

Big Black

Kosciusko
Louisville

MISSISSIPPI

Deer Creek

Yazoo City
Carthage
Philadelphia
MISSISSIPPI CHOCTAW INDIAN RESERVATION

Mississippi Petrified Forest
Ross Barnett Reservoir
Pearl

Ridgeland
Meridian

Vicksburg
Forest

Jackson
Brandon
Newton

Leaf

Crystal Springs
Quitman

Chickasawhay

Hazlehurst
Magee

Collins
Waynesboro

Natchez
Brookhaven
Ellisville

Pearl

Homochitto

McComb
Columbia
Hattiesburg

Leaf

Centreville

Lucedale

Black Creek

Wiggins

Pascagoula

Gulfport
Biloxi

Bay St. Louis
Pascagoula

Mississippi Sound

Mississippi

GULF OF MEXICO

Tennessee

Highest point in Mississippi

NORTH CAROLINA

LAND & WATER Mount Mitchell, Lake Norman, and the Cape Fear River are important land and water features of North Carolina.

STATEHOOD North Carolina became the 12th state in 1789.

PEOPLE & PLACES North Carolina's population is 10,383,620. Raleigh is the state capital. The largest city is Charlotte.

FUN FACT The University of North Carolina, the first public university in the United States, opened its doors in 1795 with two professors and 41 students.

Highest point in North Carolina and east of the Mississippi

TENNESSEE

•Boone

Mt. Mitchell
6,684 ft
2,037 m

Catawb•

GREAT SMOKY MOUNTAINS NATIONAL PARK

Hickory•

Great Smoky Mts.

•Asheville

Fontana L.

EASTERN CHEROKEE I.R.

•Franklin

APPALACHIAN MOUNTA

Blue R i

Chattooga

GEORGIA

SOUTH

The chapel tower is a landmark on the campus of Duke University in Durham.

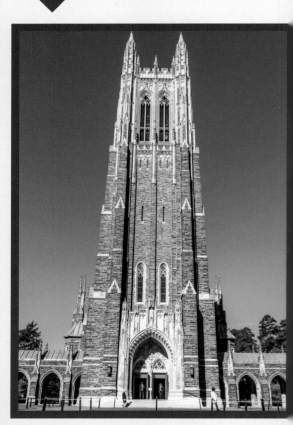

North Carolina State Flag

MAY 20TH 1775
N ★ C
APRIL 12TH 1776

Cardinal
State Bird

Flowering Dogwood
State Flower

Basketball is a popular sport among all ages in North Carolina, whether on the court or in the backyard.

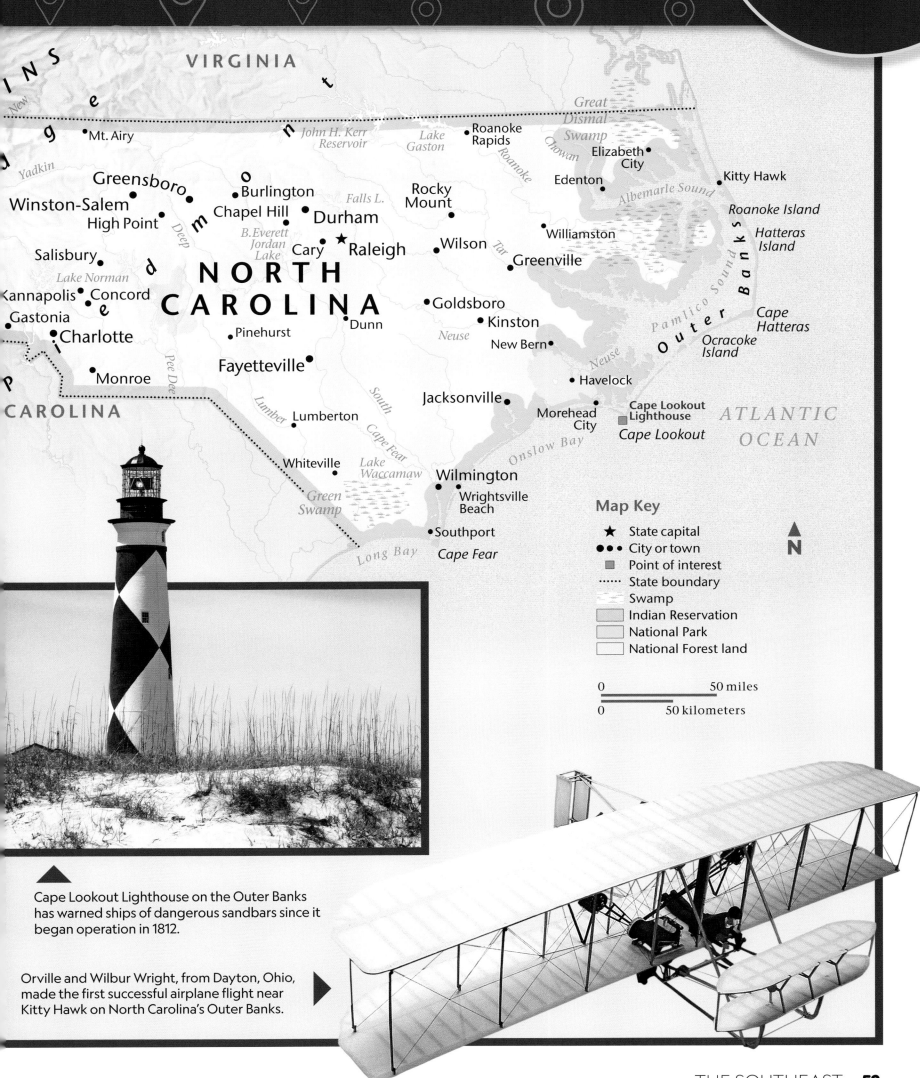

VIRGINIA

Mt. Airy

New

Yadkin

Greensboro

Winston-Salem

High Point

Salisbury

Lake Norman

Kannapolis • Concord

Gastonia

• Charlotte

• Monroe

CAROLINA

Deep

Pee Dee

Burlington

Chapel Hill

B. Everett Jordan Lake

Cary

Pinehurst

• Dunn

Fayetteville

Lumber

Lumberton

Whiteville

Green Swamp

Lake Waccamaw

South

Cape Fear

Falls L.

Durham

★ Raleigh

NORTH CAROLINA

Goldsboro

• Kinston

Neuse

New Bern •

Long Bay

John H. Kerr Reservoir

Lake Gaston

Rocky Mount

• Wilson

Tar

Greenville

Williamston •

Roanoke Rapids

Roanoke

Great Dismal Swamp

Chowan

Edenton

Elizabeth City

Albemarle Sound

Kitty Hawk

Roanoke Island

Hatteras Island

Pamlico Sound

Outer Banks

Cape Hatteras

Ocracoke Island

Neuse

• Havelock

Jacksonville •

Morehead City

■ Cape Lookout Lighthouse

Cape Lookout

ATLANTIC OCEAN

Onslow Bay

Wilmington

• Wrightsville Beach

• Southport

Cape Fear

Map Key

★ State capital

••• City or town

■ Point of interest

..... State boundary

  Swamp

  Indian Reservation

  National Park

  National Forest land

N

0   50 miles

0   50 kilometers

▲ Cape Lookout Lighthouse on the Outer Banks has warned ships of dangerous sandbars since it began operation in 1812.

Orville and Wilbur Wright, from Dayton, Ohio, made the first successful airplane flight near ▶ Kitty Hawk on North Carolina's Outer Banks.

SOUTH CAROLINA

SOUTH CAROLINA

 LAND & WATER Sumter National Forest, Lake Marion, and the Great Pee Dee River are important land and water features of South Carolina.

 STATEHOOD South Carolina became the 8th state in 1788.

 PEOPLE & PLACES South Carolina's population is 5,084,127. Columbia is the state capital. The largest city is Charleston.

 FUN FACT Sweetgrass baskets have been made in the coastal lowland region for more than 300 years. They were originally used in the planting and processing of rice.

South Carolina State Flag

Yellow Jessamine
State Flower

Carolina Wren
State Bird

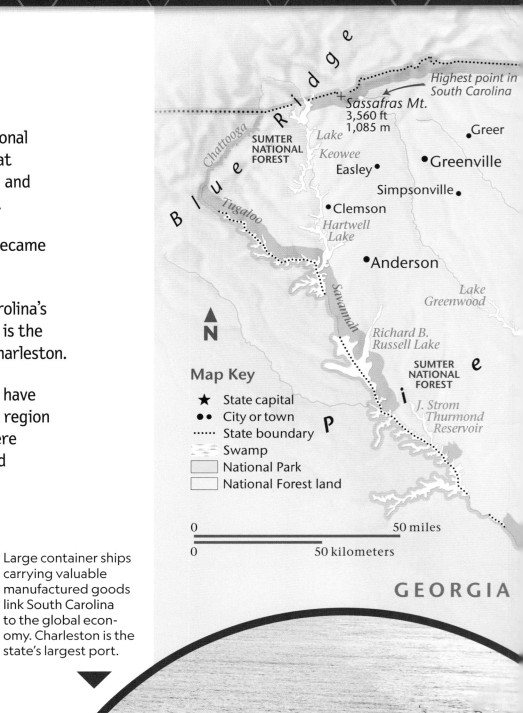

Blue Ridge

Chattooga

Tugaloo

Highest point in South Carolina

+ Sassafras Mt. 3,560 ft 1,085 m

SUMTER NATIONAL FOREST

Lake Keowee

Easley •

Hartwell Lake

Savannah

• Greer

• Greenville

Simpsonville •

• Clemson

• Anderson

Lake Greenwood

Richard B. Russell Lake

SUMTER NATIONAL FOREST

J. Strom Thurmond Reservoir

N

Map Key

★ State capital
•• City or town
...... State boundary
Swamp
National Park
National Forest land

0   50 miles
0   50 kilometers

GEORGIA

Large container ships carrying valuable manufactured goods link South Carolina to the global economy. Charleston is the state's largest port.

NORTH CAROLINA

Gaffney
Spartanburg
York
Rock Hill
Union
Lancaster
Cheraw

Wylie Lake
Broad
Catawba

SUMTER
NATIONAL
FOREST

*Wateree
Lake*
Wateree

Winnsboro
Newberry
Dillon
Darlington
Florence

Saluda
*Lake
Murray*
Irmo

S O U T H

West Columbia ★ Columbia
Sumter

Congaree
Lake City
Loris

CONGAREE
NATIONAL PARK

Little Pee Dee
Great Pee Dee

C A R O L I N A

Myrtle Beach

Long Bay

Aiken
S. Fork Edisto
N. Fork Edisto
Orangeburg
Black

Williston
*Lake
Marion*
Santee
Georgetown

Bamberg
*Lake
Moultrie*

Edisto
Moncks Corner
Cooper

North
Island

Allendale
Summerville

Walterboro
North
Charleston
Mount
Pleasant

Cape Island

Savannah

Charleston

A T L A N T I C

O C E A N

*Edisto
Island*

Beaufort
*St. Helena
Sound*

St. Helena
Island
Parris Island

Port Royal Sound

Hilton Head
Island
Hilton Head
Island
Daufuskie Island

Hard-packed sands on a Hilton Head Island beach are perfect for a family bicycle outing.

Loggerhead turtles, which are an endangered species, lay their eggs in nests that they dig in the sand in the coastal area known as the Lowcountry.

TENNESSEE

TENNESSEE

 LAND & WATER The Cumberland Plateau, Reelfoot Lake, and the Tennessee River are important land and water features of Tennessee.

 STATEHOOD Tennessee became the 16th state in 1796.

 PEOPLE & PLACES Tennessee's population is 6,770,010. Nashville/Davidson County is the state capital and the largest city.

 FUN FACT In 1811–1812 three major earthquakes, known as the New Madrid earthquakes, changed the landscape in parts of Tennessee and neighboring Missouri. The ground in northwest Tennessee sank, creating Reelfoot Lake.

Tennessee State Flag

Iris
State Flower

Mockingbird
State Bird

MISSOURI
Kentucky Lake
Lake Barkley
Mississippi
Reelfoot L.
• Union City
Obion
• Martin • Paris
Tennessee
• Dyersburg
ARKANSAS
T
Duck
• Jackson
Buffalo
Mississippi
Bartlett
• Savannah •
Hatchie
• Memphis
Pickwick Lake
Germantown • • Collierville
Tennessee
MISSISSIPPI

Memphis is famous for its barbecue, especially baby back ribs that are cooked so long that the meat falls from the bones.

Norris Dam, on a tributary of the Tennessee River, was completed in 1936. It was constructed to generate electricity.

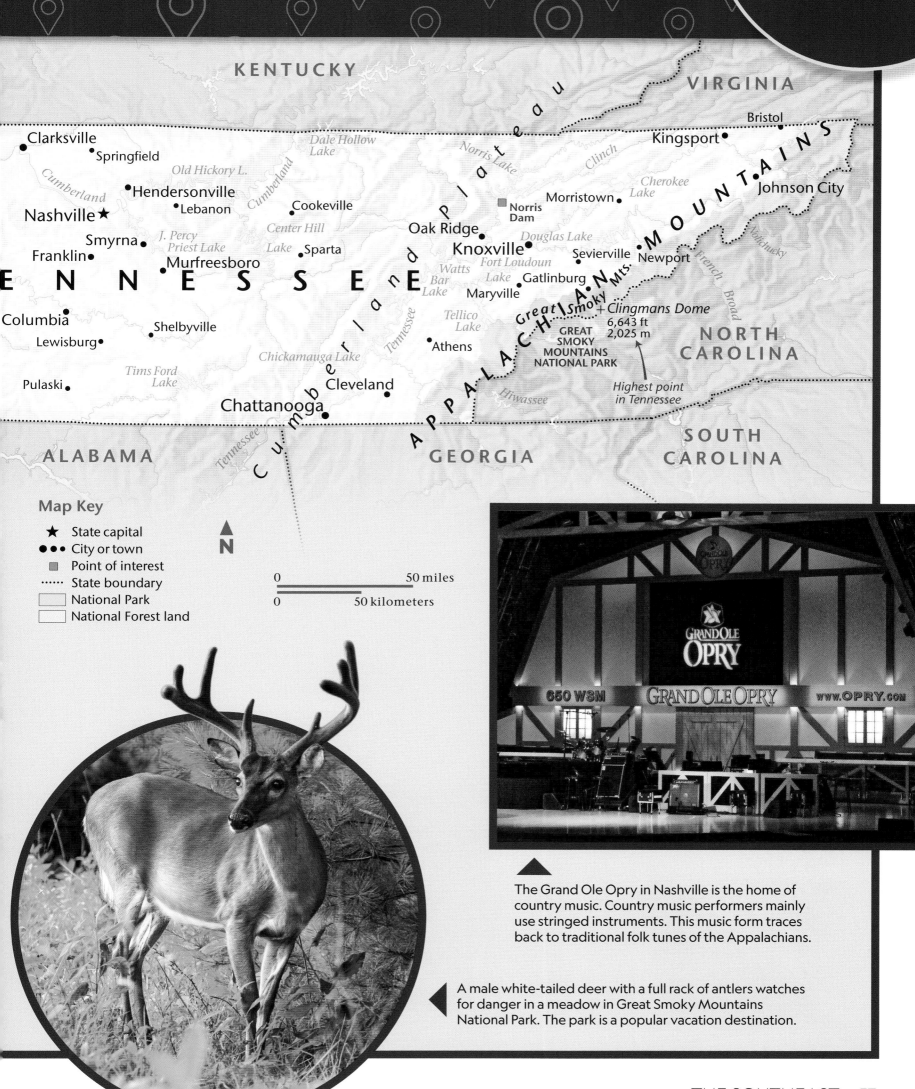

KENTUCKY

VIRGINIA

Bristol

Kingsport

Clarksville

Springfield

Dale Hollow Lake

Norris Lake

Clinch

Johnson City

Cherokee Lake

Old Hickory L.

Cumberland

Cumberland

Cookeville

Morristown

Hendersonville

Lebanon

APPALACHIAN MOUNTAINS

Nashville ★

Center Hill Lake

Norris Dam

Oak Ridge

Great Smoky Mts.

Smyrna

J. Percy Priest Lake

Sparta

Knoxville

Douglas Lake

Sevierville

Newport

French Broad

Franklin

Murfreesboro

Fort Loudoun Lake

Gatlinburg

Nolichucky

Watts Bar Lake

Maryville

Clingmans Dome
6,643 ft
2,025 m

Columbia

Tellico Lake

NORTH CAROLINA

Shelbyville

Tennessee

Athens

GREAT SMOKY MOUNTAINS NATIONAL PARK

Lewisburg

Chickamauga Lake

Great

Highest point in Tennessee

Tims Ford Lake

Cleveland

Pulaski

Chattanooga

Hiwassee

SOUTH CAROLINA

ENNESSEE

Cumberland Plateau

ALABAMA

Tennessee

GEORGIA

Map Key

★ State capital
●●● City or town
■ Point of interest
⋯⋯ State boundary
☐ National Park
☐ National Forest land

N

0   50 miles
0   50 kilometers

▲ The Grand Ole Opry in Nashville is the home of country music. Country music performers mainly use stringed instruments. This music form traces back to traditional folk tunes of the Appalachians.

◄ A male white-tailed deer with a full rack of antlers watches for danger in a meadow in Great Smoky Mountains National Park. The park is a popular vacation destination.

VIRGINIA

VIRGINIA

LAND & WATER The Blue Ridge mountains, Shenandoah National Park, and the James River are important land and water features of Virginia.

STATEHOOD Virginia became the 10th state in 1788.

PEOPLE & PLACES Virginia's population is 8,517,685. Richmond is the state capital. The largest city is Virginia Beach.

FUN FACT Eight U.S. presidents—Washington, Jefferson, Madison, Monroe, Harrison, Tyler, Taylor, and Wilson—were born in Virginia, more than in any other state.

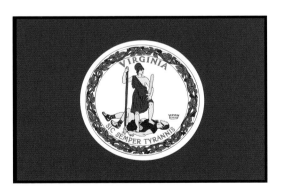

Virginia State Flag

An old barn, bales of hay, and trees in autumn foliage are a common sight in the Appalachian Mountains of Virginia.

KENTUCKY

Bluefield

Alleghe

Clinch

Big Stone Gap

Clinch Mt.

North Fork

Marion

Powell

Bristol

Holston

S. Fork

APPALA

Mt. Rogers
5,729 ft
1,746 m

Highest point in Virginia

TENNESSEE

In Williamsburg, an early capital of Virginia, a fife and drum band maintains the tradition of military music as it marches down a street.

Flowering Dogwood
State Flower

Cardinal
State Bird

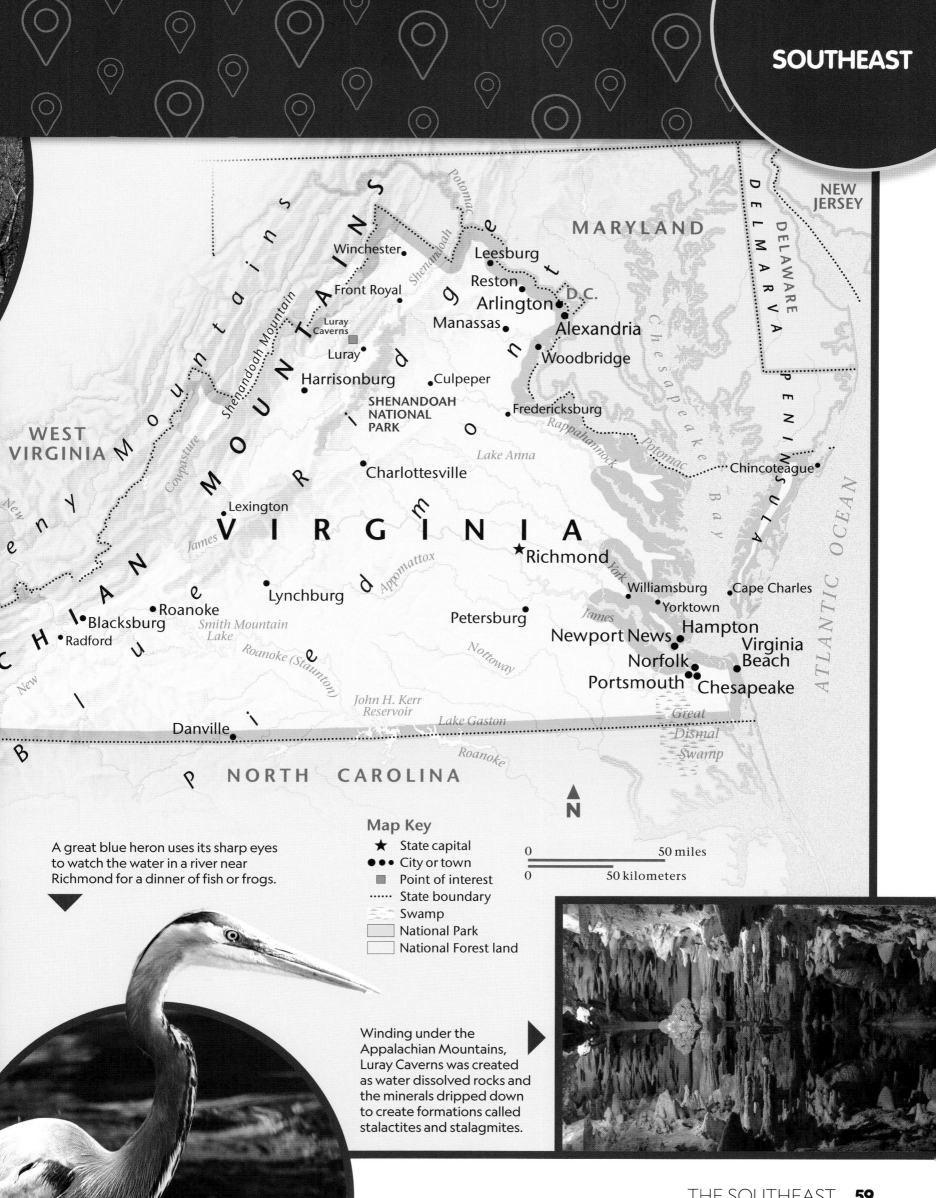

NEW JERSEY

MARYLAND

DELAWARE

DELMARVA PENINSULA

Potomac

Winchester
Leesburg
Reston
Front Royal
Arlington
D.C.
Luray Caverns
Manassas
Alexandria
Luray
Woodbridge
Harrisonburg
Culpeper

SHENANDOAH NATIONAL PARK

Fredericksburg

Shenandoah

Shenandoah Mountain

WEST VIRGINIA

Compasture

Rappahannock

Lake Anna

Chincoteague

Charlottesville

Chesapeake Bay

Lexington

Potomac

James

VIRGINIA

New

Richmond

Williamsburg
Cape Charles
Yorktown

Appomattox

York

Lynchburg

Petersburg

Smith Mountain Lake

Roanoke
Blacksburg
Radford

James

Hampton
Newport News
Virginia Beach
Norfolk
Portsmouth
Chesapeake

Nottoway

New

Roanoke (Staunton)

ATLANTIC OCEAN

John H. Kerr Reservoir

Great Dismal Swamp

Danville

Lake Gaston

Roanoke

NORTH CAROLINA

N

A great blue heron uses its sharp eyes to watch the water in a river near Richmond for a dinner of fish or frogs.

Map Key

★ State capital
●●● City or town
■ Point of interest
···· State boundary
Swamp
National Park
National Forest land

0 ———————— 50 miles
0 ———————— 50 kilometers

Winding under the Appalachian Mountains, Luray Caverns was created as water dissolved rocks and the minerals dripped down to create formations called stalactites and stalagmites.

WEST VIRGINIA

WEST VIRGINIA

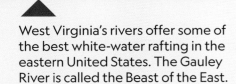

LAND & WATER
The Allegheny Mountains, the Ohio River, and the New River are important land and water features of West Virginia.

STATEHOOD West Virginia
became the 35th state in 1863.

PEOPLE & PLACES
West Virginia's population is 1,805,832. Charleston is the state capital and the largest city.

FUN FACT One of the oldest
and largest burial mounds is located in Moundsville along the Ohio River. Built by the Adena people, the mound is more than 2,000 years old.

West Virginia's rivers offer some of the best white-water rafting in the eastern United States. The Gauley River is called the Beast of the East.

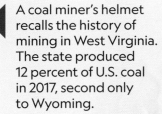

A coal miner's helmet recalls the history of mining in West Virginia. The state produced 12 percent of U.S. coal in 2017, second only to Wyoming.

Foliage turns red in the Dolly Sods Wilderness in the Monongahela National Forest. The area is named for an early settler family.

Point Pleasant

Ohio

KENTUCKY   Huntington

Big Sandy

Guyandotte

West Virginia State Flag

Tug Fork

Williamson

Rhododendron
State Flower

Cardinal
State Bird

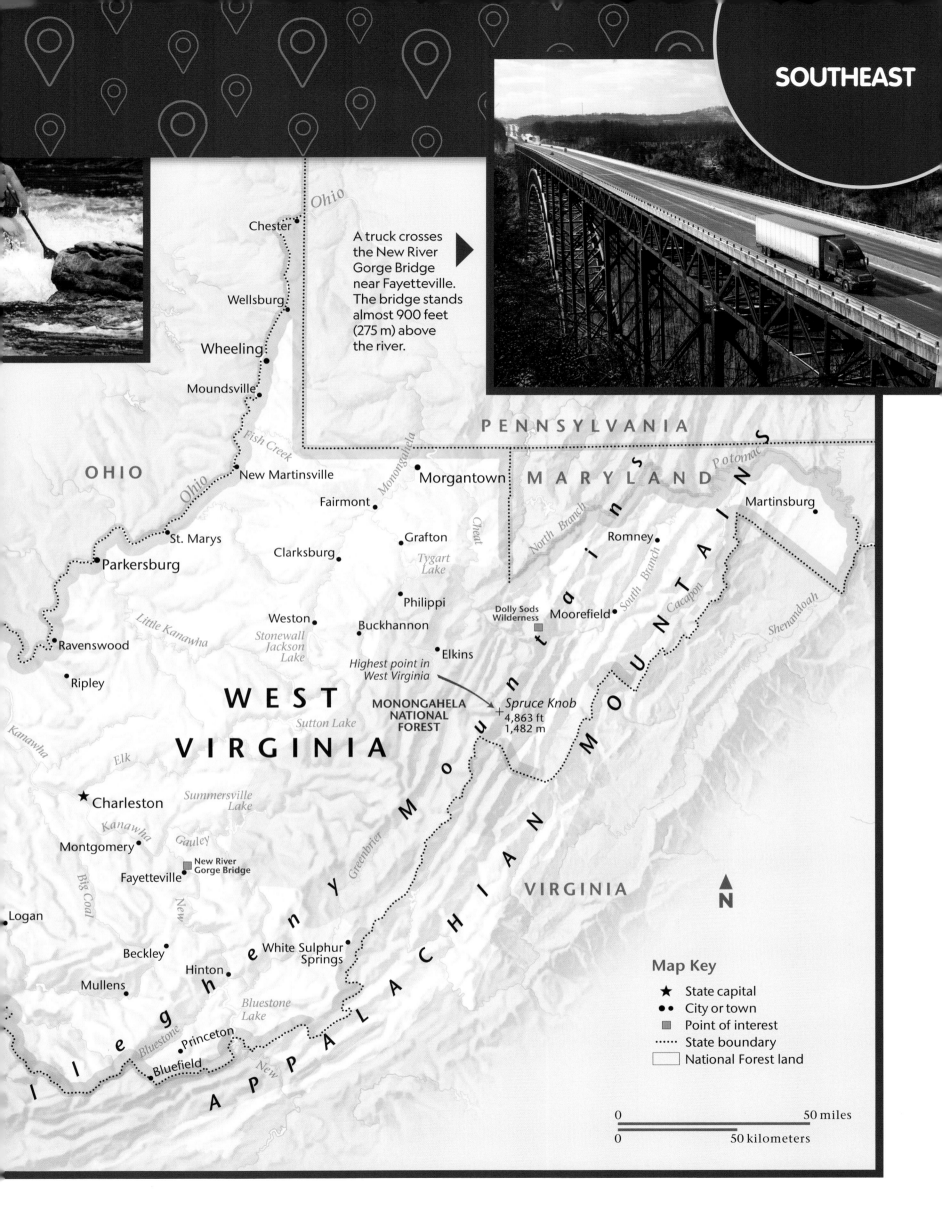

A truck crosses the New River Gorge Bridge near Fayetteville. The bridge stands almost 900 feet (275 m) above the river. ▶

OHIO

PENNSYLVANIA

MARYLAND

Ohio

Chester

Wellsburg

Wheeling

Moundsville

Fish Creek

New Martinsville

Morgantown

Monongahela

Fairmont

Cheat

Grafton

Ohio

St. Marys

Clarksburg

Tygart Lake

Martinsburg

Romney

North Branch

Potomac

South Branch

Cacapon

Parkersburg

Philippi

Dolly Sods Wilderness

Moorefield

Little Kanawha

Weston

Buckhannon

Shenandoah

Stonewall Jackson Lake

Ravenswood

Elkins

Highest point in West Virginia

Ripley

WEST VIRGINIA

MONONGAHELA NATIONAL FOREST

Spruce Knob
4,863 ft
1,482 m

Sutton Lake

Kanawha

★ Charleston

Summersville Lake

Kanawha

Elk

Gauley

Montgomery

New River Gorge Bridge

Fayetteville

New

Big Coal

Greenbrier

VIRGINIA

N

Logan

Beckley

White Sulphur Springs

Hinton

Mullens

Bluestone Lake

Map Key

★ State capital

•• City or town

■ Point of interest

⋯ State boundary

☐ National Forest land

Bluestone

Princeton

Bluefield

New

APPALACHIAN MOUNTAINS

Allegheny Mountains

0 _____ 50 miles

0 _____ 50 kilometers

THE MIDWEST

The Midwest is a region of prairies, lakes, and rivers. The Mississippi River and its tributaries drain America's interior. The region supports some of the most productive agriculture in the world, including the crops corn, wheat, and soybeans. Industries such as food processing, steel, and automobile production led to the growth of cities such as Chicago, Illinois, and Detroit, Michigan, but these industries are now being replaced by technology and information-based businesses.

Dairy cows are an important part of the region's economy. The Midwest supplies much of the country's milk, cheese, and butter.

White clouds float across a blue sky above this flowering Kansas prairie. The Midwest is a major grain-producing region.

ILLINOIS

 The Pilsen neighborhood on Chicago's lower west side is known for its colorful street murals. This painting celebrates women in the multicultural population of this immigrant neighborhood.

LAND & WATER
The Shawnee National Forest, the Illinois River, and Lake Michigan are important land and water features of Illinois.

STATEHOOD Illinois
became the 21st state in 1818.

PEOPLE & PLACES
Illinois has a population of 12,741,080. Springfield is the state capital. The largest city is Chicago.

FUN FACT The Chicago River
is dyed green on St. Patrick's Day to honor Chicago's large Irish population. The formula for the green dye is a closely kept secret.

Pig races are a fun-filled highlight of the annual Illinois State Fair in Springfield.

Illinois State Flag

Violet
State Flower

Cardinal
State Bird

WRIGLEY FIELD
HOME OF
CHICAGO CUB

PIRATES   TOP 9TH   CUB
1   4

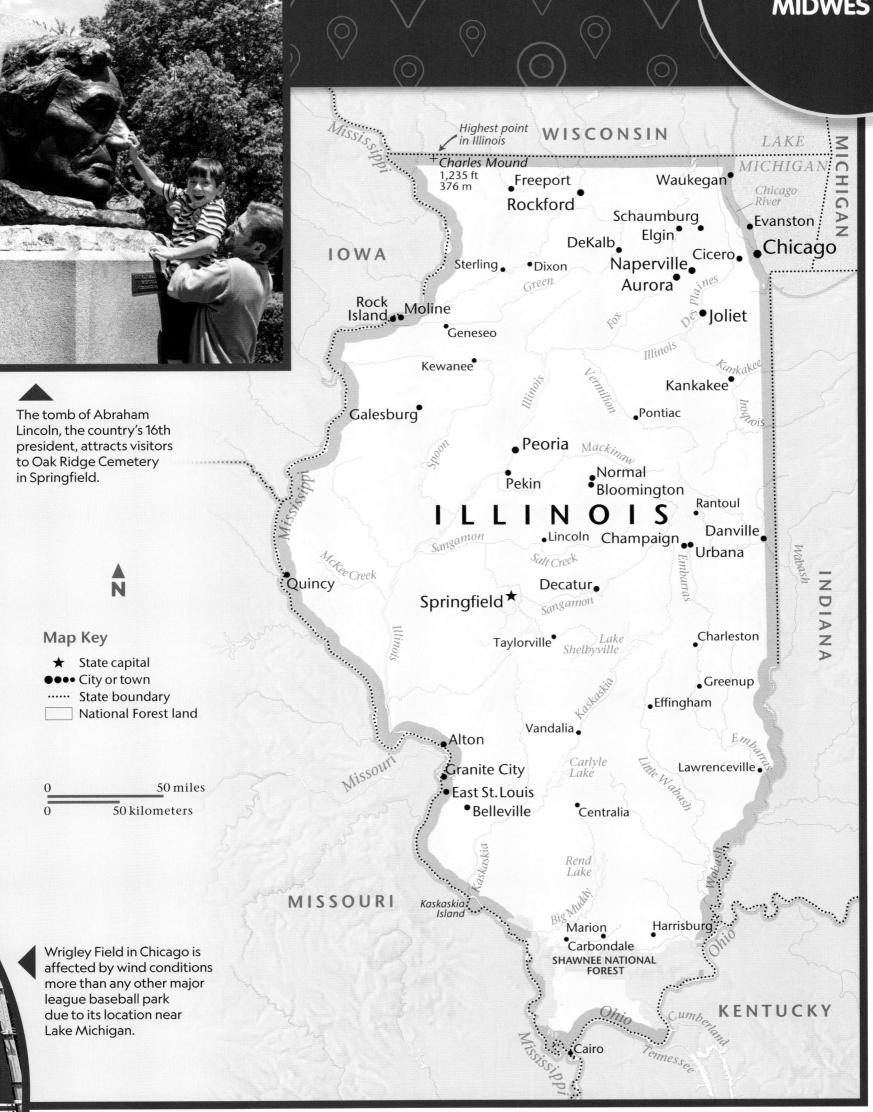

The tomb of Abraham Lincoln, the country's 16th president, attracts visitors to Oak Ridge Cemetery in Springfield.

N

Map Key
★ State capital
●●●● City or town
⋯⋯ State boundary
▢ National Forest land

0 ————— 50 miles
0 ————— 50 kilometers

Wrigley Field in Chicago is affected by wind conditions more than any other major league baseball park due to its location near Lake Michigan.

WISCONSIN

Mississippi

Highest point in Illinois
✛ Charles Mound
1,235 ft
376 m

LAKE MICHIGAN

Chicago River

MICHIGAN

Freeport
Rockford
Waukegan

IOWA

Schaumburg
Elgin
Evanston

DeKalb
Cicero
Chicago

Sterling
Dixon
Naperville
Aurora

Green

Fox

Des Plaines

Joliet

Rock Island
Moline
Geneseo

Illinois

Kewanee

Vermilion

Illinois

Kankakee

Kankakee

Iroquois

Galesburg

Pontiac

Spoon

Peoria
Mackinaw

Pekin
Normal
Bloomington

Rantoul

I L L I N O I S

Danville

Sangamon
Lincoln
Champaign
Urbana

Salt Creek

Embarras

Quincy

McKee Creek

Decatur
Sangamon

Mississippi

Springfield ★

Charleston

Illinois

Taylorville
Lake Shelbyville

Greenup

Kaskaskia

Effingham

Vandalia

Embarras

Alton
Carlyle Lake

Lawrenceville

Granite City

Missouri

East St. Louis
Belleville

Centralia

Little Wabash

Wabash

INDIANA

MISSOURI

Kaskaskia

Rend Lake

Kaskaskia Island

Big Muddy

Marion
Harrisburg

Carbondale

Ohio

SHAWNEE NATIONAL FOREST

KENTUCKY

Ohio
Cumberland

Mississippi
Cairo

Tennessee

INDIANA

INDIANA

 LAND & WATER
The Hoosier National Forest, Lake Michigan, and the Wabash River are important land and water features of Indiana.

 STATEHOOD Indiana became the 19th state in 1816.

 PEOPLE & PLACES
Indiana's population is 6,691,878. Indianapolis is the state capital and the largest city.

 FUN FACT The intersection of U.S. Highway 40 and U.S. Highway 41, at Wabash Avenue and Seventh Street in Terre Haute, is called the Crossroads of America.

Indiana State Flag

Peony
State Flower

Cardinal
State Bird

The Indianapolis Motor Speedway is the largest sports stadium in the world. It has more than 250,000 permanent seats and hosts the famous Indy 500 race.

The Hoosiers of Indiana University, in Bloomington, are part of the powerful Big Ten Conference in college football. Sports are an important tradition and a favorite pastime in Indiana.

A boy gathers sweet corn on a family farm near Centerville. Corn is an important food for both people and livestock.

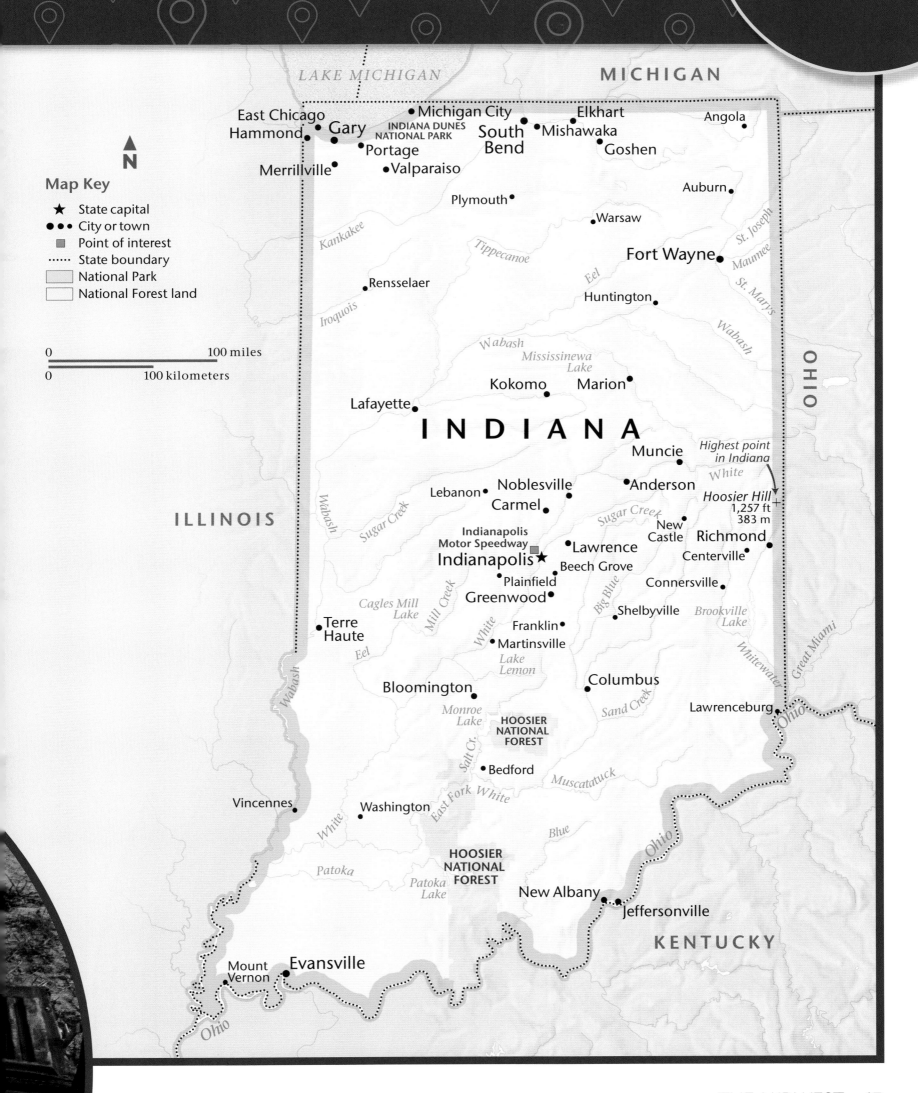

Map Key
- ★ State capital
- •• City or town
- ■ Point of interest
- ···· State boundary
- National Park
- National Forest land

0   100 miles
0   100 kilometers

LAKE MICHIGAN

MICHIGAN

East Chicago
Hammond
Gary
Merrillville
Portage
Michigan City
INDIANA DUNES NATIONAL PARK
Valparaiso
South Bend
Mishawaka
Elkhart
Goshen
Angola
Auburn
Plymouth
Warsaw
Fort Wayne
Huntington
Rensselaer

Kankakee
Iroquois
Tippecanoe
Eel
St. Joseph
Maumee
St. Mary's
Wabash

ILLINOIS

Wabash
Mississinewa Lake
Kokomo
Marion

INDIANA

Lafayette

Muncie
Highest point in Indiana
White
Lebanon
Noblesville
Carmel
Anderson
Sugar Creek
Hoosier Hill
1,257 ft
383 m
New Castle
Richmond
Centerville

OHIO

Indianapolis Motor Speedway
Indianapolis
Lawrence
Beech Grove
Plainfield
Greenwood
Franklin
Martinsville
Lake Lemon
Connersville
Shelbyville
Big Blue
Brookville Lake

Cagles Mill Lake
Mill Creek
White
Eel
Terre Haute

Columbus
Sand Creek
Lawrenceburg
Ohio
Great Miami
Whitewater

Bloomington
Monroe Lake
HOOSIER NATIONAL FOREST
Salt Cr.
Bedford
Muscatatuck

Vincennes
Washington
East Fork White
Blue

White
Patoka
HOOSIER NATIONAL FOREST
Patoka Lake
New Albany
Jeffersonville
Ohio

KENTUCKY

Mount Vernon
Evansville
Ohio

IOWA

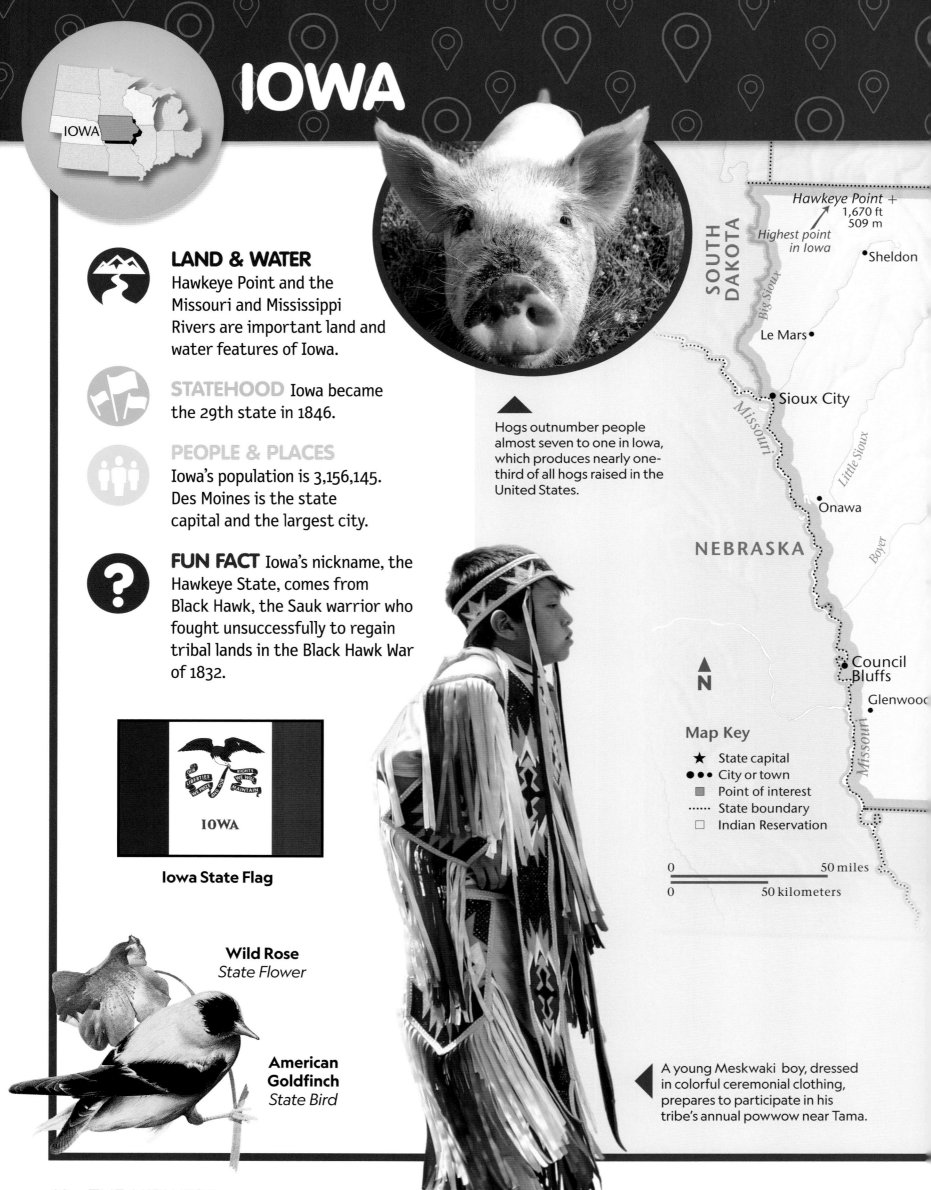

LAND & WATER
Hawkeye Point and the Missouri and Mississippi Rivers are important land and water features of Iowa.

STATEHOOD
Iowa became the 29th state in 1846.

PEOPLE & PLACES
Iowa's population is 3,156,145. Des Moines is the state capital and the largest city.

FUN FACT
Iowa's nickname, the Hawkeye State, comes from Black Hawk, the Sauk warrior who fought unsuccessfully to regain tribal lands in the Black Hawk War of 1832.

Iowa State Flag

Wild Rose
State Flower

American Goldfinch
State Bird

Hogs outnumber people almost seven to one in Iowa, which produces nearly one-third of all hogs raised in the United States.

Hawkeye Point + 1,670 ft 509 m
Highest point in Iowa

SOUTH DAKOTA

NEBRASKA

Big Sioux

Missouri

Little Sioux

Boyer

Missouri

• Sheldon
Le Mars •
• Sioux City
• Onawa
• Council Bluffs
• Glenwood

N

Map Key
★ State capital
●●● City or town
■ Point of interest
•••• State boundary
□ Indian Reservation

0   50 miles
0   50 kilometers

A young Meskwaki boy, dressed in colorful ceremonial clothing, prepares to participate in his tribe's annual powwow near Tama.

MINNESOTA

WISCONSIN

Spencer
Emmetsburg
Forest City
Mason City
Osage
Charles City
New Hampton
Effigy Mounds Nat. Mon.
Marquette

Storm Lake
Humboldt
Waverly
Oelwein

Fort Dodge
Webster City
Cedar Falls
Waterloo
Manchester
Dubuque

Des Moines (river)
Raccoon
Iowa (river)

I O W A

Monticello

Denison
Jefferson
Ames
Marshalltown
Meskwaki I.R.
Tama
Cedar Rapids
Maquoketa

Perry
Clinton

Harlan
Ankeny
Newton
Iowa City
Bettendorf
Davenport

Urbandale
★ Des Moines
West Des Moines

Atlantic

Indianola
Lake Red Rock
Pella
Washington

Oskaloosa

Thompson

Red Oak

Chariton
Rathbun Lake
Ottumwa
Mount Pleasant

ILLINOIS

Burlington

Clarinda
Centerville
Bloomfield

Des Moines (river)

MISSOURI

Keokuk

Mississippi
Wapsipinicon
Upper Iowa
Shell Rock
Cedar
Turkey
Iowa
Cedar

Effigy Mounds National Monument, near Marquette, preserves 206 sacred mounds created by Eastern Woodland tribes more than 1,000 years ago.

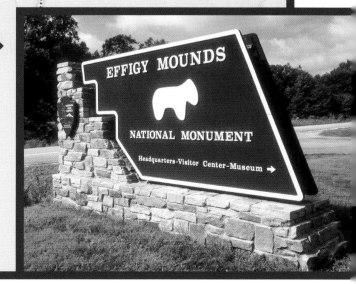

EFFIGY MOUNDS NATIONAL MONUMENT
Headquarters-Visitor Center-Museum →

◀ Paper-thin sheets of 23-karat gold cover the central dome of the state capitol building in Des Moines.

KANSAS

KANSAS

LAND & WATER Mount Sunflower, the Flint Hills, and the Missouri River are important land and water features of Kansas.

STATEHOOD Kansas became the 34th state in 1861.

PEOPLE & PLACES The population of Kansas is 2,911,505. Topeka is the state capital. The largest city is Wichita.

? **FUN FACT** Pizza Hut, the world's largest pizza chain, opened its first restaurant in Wichita in 1958. Today the company has more than 16,900 restaurants in at least 105 countries.

Kansas State Flag

▲ A statue of the Tin Man, a character from *The Wonderful Wizard of Oz,* the popular fantasy book partly set in Kansas, sits in a garden.

Map Key

N

★ State capital
●●● City or town
■ Point of interest
····· State boundary
▢ Indian Reservation

0   50 miles
0   50 kilometers

COLORADO

HIGH PLAINS

Goodland •Colby
Highest point in Kansas
Oakley•
+ Mt. Sunflower
4,039 ft
1,231 m

Arkansas Lakin•   Garden City•

Ulysses•

Cimarron

Monument Rocks, located south of Oakley, were once part of an ancient inland seabed. Over millions of years, erosion by wind and water has created these chalk formations. ▼

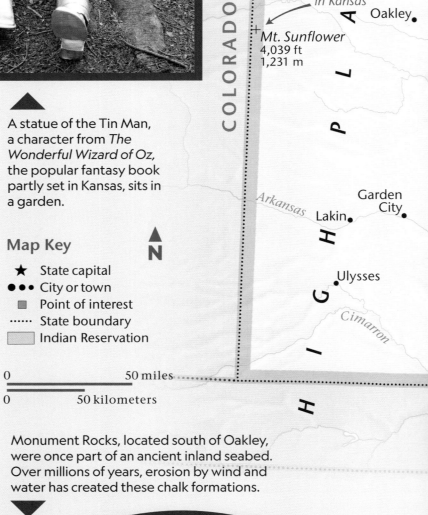

Sunflower
State Flower

Western Meadowlark
State Bird

NEBRASKA

Norton
Phillipsburg
Belleville
Prairie Dog Creek
North Fork Solomon
Concordia
Clay
Center
*Tuttle
Creek
Lake*
Seneca
SAC AND FOX
I.R.
IOWA
I.R.
Hiawatha
KICKAPOO
I.R.
Missouri
South Fork Solomon
Beloit
Holton
Atchison
Fort
Leavenworth
POTAWATOMI
I.R.
*Perry
Lake*
Plainville
Solomon
Republican
Manhattan
Wamego
Leavenworth
S m o k y   H i l l s
*Milford
Lake*
Kansas
Kansas City
WaKeeney
Saline
Abilene
Junction City
Topeka ★
Overland Park
Monument
Rocks
Russell
Salina
Smoky Hill
Lawrence
Olathe
Smoky Hill

K A N S A S

Cheyenne Bottoms
Osage City
Osawatomie
Missouri
Ness City
Walnut Creek
Great Bend
Arkansas
Emporia
*John Redmond
Reservoir*
Marais des Cygnes
*Marion
Lake*
Hesston
Newton
Verdigris
Burlington
Buckner Creek
Hutchinson
*El Dorado
Lake*
F l i n t   H i l l s
Fort Scott
Dodge City
*Cheney
Reservoir*
El Dorado
Chanute
Neosho
Pratt
Kingman
Wichita
Elk
*Elk City
Lake*
Parsons
Greensburg
R e d   H i l l s
Medicine Lodge
Medicine
Lodge
Walnut
Independence
Cimarron
Arkansas
Arkansas
City
Caney
Coffeyville

M I S S O U R I

OKLAHOMA

Tornadoes, massive twisting storm systems, are a frequent occurrence in the south-central plains of the U.S. Known as Tornado Alley, this area, which includes Kansas, most commonly experiences these violent storms between April and June.

MICHIGAN

MICHIGAN

A statue of Austin Blair, governor of Michigan during the Civil War, stands in front of the state capitol in Lansing.

 LAND & WATER The Upper and Lower Peninsulas and Lakes Superior, Michigan, and Huron are important land and water features of Michigan.

 STATEHOOD Michigan became the 26th state in 1837.

 PEOPLE & PLACES Michigan's population is 9,995,915. Lansing is the state capital. The largest city is Detroit.

 FUN FACT The Detroit River is home to the only floating post office in the United States. Operating since 1874, the post office, which even has its own zip code, is located on a tugboat.

Boys explore nature's wonders on the bank of a river near Niles. The town sits on the site of Fort St. Joseph, built by the French in 1691.

Michigan State Flag

The Straits of Mackinac join Lakes Michigan and Huron. Crossing the straits, the five-mile (8-km)-long Mackinac Bridge connects Michigan's Upper Peninsula to the southern part of the state.

Apple Blossom
State Flower

Robin
State Bird

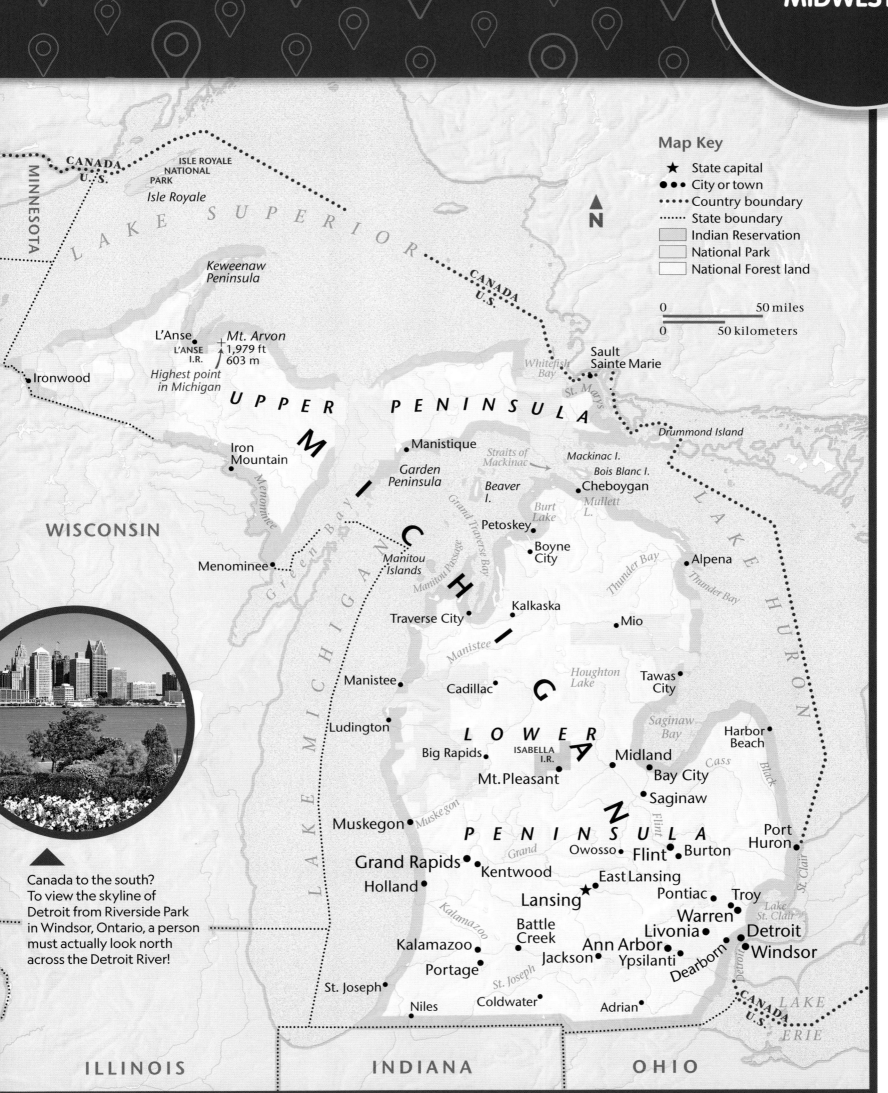

Map Key

★ State capital
●●● City or town
••••• Country boundary
••••• State boundary
▢ Indian Reservation
▢ National Park
▢ National Forest land

0   50 miles
0   50 kilometers

MINNESOTA

CANADA
U.S.

ISLE ROYALE
NATIONAL
PARK
Isle Royale

LAKE SUPERIOR

*Keweenaw
Peninsula*

CANADA
U.S.

L'Anse
L'ANSE
I.R.
Mt. Arvon
1,979 ft
603 m
*Highest point
in Michigan*

Ironwood

Sault
Sainte Marie

*Whitefish
Bay*

St. Marys

U P P E R   P E N I N S U L A

Drummond Island

M I C H I G A N

Iron
Mountain

Manistique

*Garden
Peninsula*

*Straits of
Mackinac*

Mackinac I.
Bois Blanc I.

Cheboygan

Beaver
I.

*Mullett
L.*

LAKE HURON

WISCONSIN

Menominee

Green Bay

Grand Traverse Bay

*Burt
Lake*

Petoskey

Boyne
City

Alpena

Menominee

*Manitou
Islands*

Manitou Passage

Thunder Bay

Thunder Bay

Traverse City

Kalkaska

Mio

Manistee

*Houghton
Lake*

Tawas
City

Manistee

Cadillac

G

*Saginaw
Bay*

Harbor
Beach

Ludington

L O W E R

Big Rapids

ISABELLA
I.R.

A

Midland

Cass

Black

Mt. Pleasant

Bay City

Saginaw

Muskegon

Muskegon

P E N I N S U L A

Grand

Owosso

N

Flint

Flint

Burton

Port
Huron

St. Clair

Grand Rapids

Kentwood

East Lansing

Holland

Kalamazoo

Lansing

Pontiac

Troy

Battle
Creek

Warren

Livonia

*Lake
St. Clair*

Kalamazoo

Ann Arbor

Detroit

Portage

Jackson

Ypsilanti

Windsor

Dearborn

Detroit

St. Joseph

St. Joseph

Niles

Coldwater

Adrian

CANADA
U.S.

LAKE
ERIE

ILLINOIS

INDIANA

OHIO

↑ Canada to the south?
To view the skyline of
Detroit from Riverside Park
in Windsor, Ontario, a person
must actually look north
across the Detroit River!

LAKE MICHIGAN

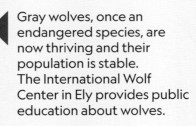

LAND & WATER Chippewa National Forest, Lake Superior, and the Mississippi River are important land and water features of Minnesota.

STATEHOOD Minnesota became the 32nd state in 1858.

PEOPLE & PLACES Minnesota's population is 5,611,179. St. Paul is the state capital. The largest city is Minneapolis.

FUN FACT Modern in-line skates were invented by two Minnesota students. Looking for a way to practice hockey in the summer, they replaced their skate blades with wheels.

Gray wolves, once an endangered species, are now thriving and their population is stable. The International Wolf Center in Ely provides public education about wolves.

Some people in Minnesota sit for hours in "ice shacks" and fish through holes cut in the ice of frozen lakes.

The skyline of Minneapolis rises above Lake Harriet, part of a popular recreation area called Chain of Lakes.

Minnesota State Flag

Showy Lady's Slipper
State Flower

Common Loon
State Bird

The "Northwest Angle" is the northernmost point in the lower 48 states

RED LAKE INDIAN RES.

CANADA
U.S.

Roseau

Hallock

Baudette

Lake of the Woods

Rainy Lake

International Falls

Rainy

VOYAGEURS NATIONAL PARK

Namakan Lake

RED LAKE INDIAN RES.

Highest point in Minnesota

CANADA
U.S.

Red River of the North

Thief River Falls

Mud Lake

Red Lake

RED LAKE INDIAN RESERVATION

Upper Red Lake

Big Fork

BOIS FORTE I.R.

Vermilion Lake

Ely

Eagle Mt. 2,301 ft 701 m

GRAND PORTAGE I.R.

Red Lake

Red Lake

Lower Red Lake

BOIS FORTE (DEER CREEK) I.R.

Grand Marais

Source of the Mississippi River

Winnibigoshish

Lake

Mississippi

CHIPPEWA NATIONAL FOREST

Mesabi Range

LEECH LAKE INDIAN RES.

LAKE SUPERIOR

Wild Rice

NORTH DAKOTA

WHITE EARTH INDIAN RESERVATION

Lake Itasca

Leech Lake

Grand Rapids

Two Harbors

MICHIGAN

Moorhead

Park Rapids

Crow Wing

FOND DU LAC I.R.

St. Louis

Duluth

Detroit Lakes

Pelican Rapids

Wadena

Mississippi

Cloquet

Proctor

Brainerd

Mille Lacs Lake

M I N N E S O T A

Sandstone

St. Croix

Bois de Sioux

Little Falls

MILLE LACS I.R.

Alexandria

Milaca

Rum

WISCONSIN

Lake Traverse

Morris

Chippewa

St. Cloud

N. Fork

Crow

Big Stone Lake

Ortonville

Benson

Litchfield

Brooklyn Park

Coon Rapids

Stillwater

SOUTH DAKOTA

Montevideo

S. Fork

Crow

Minneapolis

★ St. Paul

Hutchinson

Bloomington

Eagan

Minnesota

Redwood Falls

LOWER SIOUX I.R.

Lakeville

Red Wing

Lake Pepin

New Ulm

Mississippi

Pipestone

Mankato

Rochester

Winona

Blue Earth

St. James

Preston

Root

Fairmont

I O W A

Two Ojibwe men use sticks to harvest wild rice along the Bowstring River in the Leech Lake Indian Reservation.

Map Key

★ State capital
••• City or town
•••• Country boundary
••••• State boundary

Swamp
Indian Reservation
National Park
National Forest land

N

0   50 miles
0   50 kilometers

MISSOURI

MISSOURI

 LAND & WATER Mark Twain National Forest and the Missouri and Mississippi Rivers are important land and water features of Missouri.

 STATEHOOD Missouri became the 24th state in 1821.

 PEOPLE & PLACES Missouri's population is 6,126,452. Jefferson City is the state capital. The largest city is Kansas City.

 FUN FACT The Pony Express, established in 1860, carried letters and newspapers from St. Joseph, Missouri, to Sacramento, California, making the journey of 1,800 miles (2,897 km) in just 10 days. It ended in 1861 with the completion of the transcontinental telegraph.

Missouri State Flag

Eastern Bluebird
State Bird

Hawthorn
State Flower

The Lewis and Clark expedition, which explored the northwestern part of the Louisiana Purchase, set off from St. Charles, traveling up the Missouri River. The city celebrates the historic journey with much fanfare.

Gateway Arch, completed in 1965, recognizes the role St. Louis played in the westward expansion of the United States. Trams carry one million tourists to the top of the arch each year.

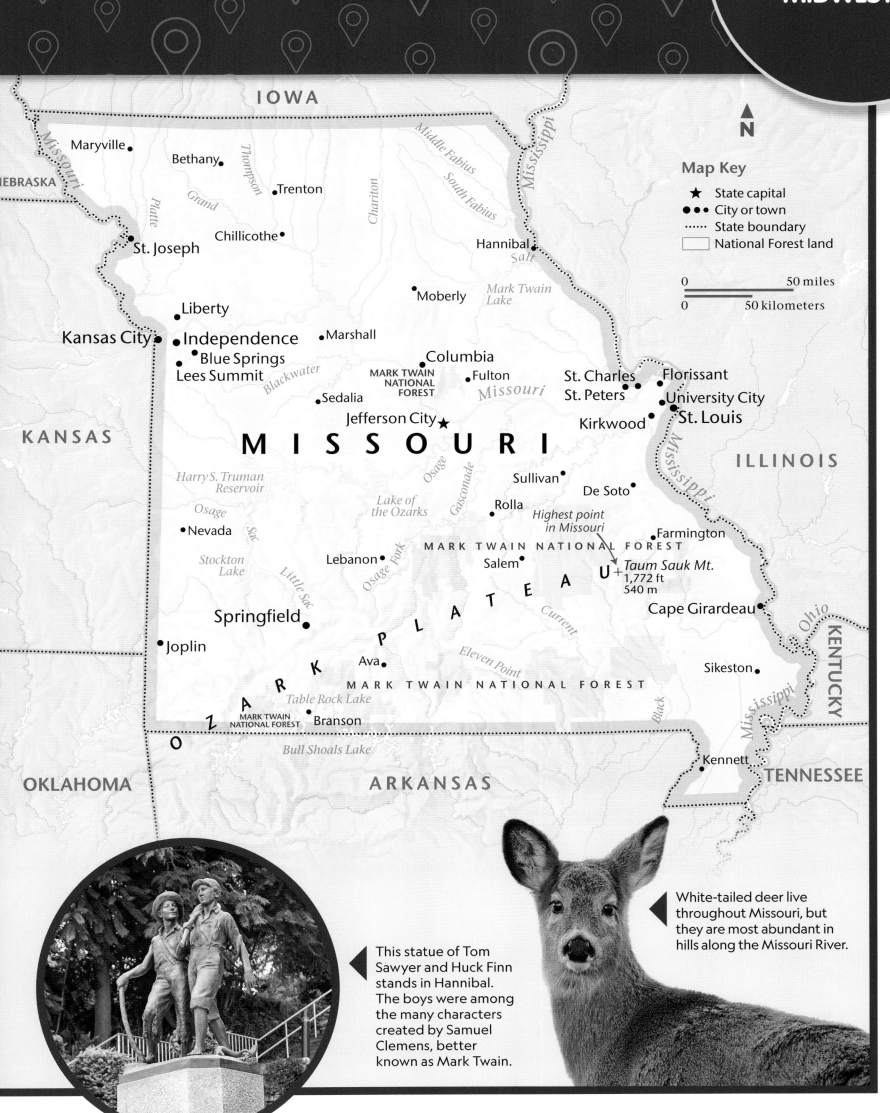

IOWA

NEBRASKA

KANSAS

OKLAHOMA

ARKANSAS

ILLINOIS

KENTUCKY

TENNESSEE

MISSOURI

Maryville
Bethany
Trenton
Chillicothe
St. Joseph
Liberty
Kansas City
Independence
Blue Springs
Lees Summit
Marshall
Sedalia
Columbia
Fulton
Jefferson City ★
Moberly
Hannibal
St. Charles
St. Peters
Florissant
University City
St. Louis
Kirkwood
Sullivan
De Soto
Rolla
Farmington
Nevada
Lebanon
Salem
Cape Girardeau
Springfield
Joplin
Ava
Sikeston
Branson
Kennett

Middle Fabius
South Fabius
Mississippi
Chariton
Thompson
Grand
Platte
Missouri
Salt
Mark Twain Lake
MARK TWAIN NATIONAL FOREST
Missouri
Blackwater
Harry S. Truman Reservoir
Osage
Lake of the Ozarks
Osage
Gasconade
Stockton Lake
Sac
Little Sac
Osage Fork
Current
MARK TWAIN NATIONAL FOREST
Eleven Point
Black
MARK TWAIN NATIONAL FOREST
Table Rock Lake
MARK TWAIN NATIONAL FOREST
Bull Shoals Lake
Mississippi
Ohio

Highest point in Missouri
Taum Sauk Mt. 1,772 ft 540 m

O Z A R K   P L A T E A U

Map Key
★ State capital
●●● City or town
••• State boundary
☐ National Forest land

0 — 50 miles
0 — 50 kilometers

N

This statue of Tom Sawyer and Huck Finn stands in Hannibal. The boys were among the many characters created by Samuel Clemens, better known as Mark Twain.

White-tailed deer live throughout Missouri, but they are most abundant in hills along the Missouri River.

NEBRASKA

NEBRASKA

LAND & WATER
The Sand Hills and the Platte and Missouri Rivers are important land and water features of Nebraska.

STATEHOOD
Nebraska became the 37th state in 1867.

PEOPLE & PLACES
Nebraska's population is 1,929,268. Lincoln is the state capital. The largest city is Omaha.

FUN FACT
The largest remaining area of original native prairie in the United States is in the Sand Hills region. It is an important stopover for migrating sandhill cranes.

Nebraska State Flag

Goldenrod
State Flower

Western Meadowlark
State Bird

Two black-tailed prairie dogs watch for signs of danger at the entrance to their burrow in the Fort Niobrara National Wildlife Refuge.

WYOMING

Crawford
White
Pine Ridge
•Gordon

Carhenge
Alliance•
S a n d

•Bayard

North Platte

Highest point in Nebraska

Kimball•
Lodgepole Cr.

Panorama Point
+ 5,426 ft
1,654 m

COLORADO

South Platte
•Ogallala

•Grant

•Imperial

Frenchman Cr.

Lake C.W.
McConaughy

P L A I N S

H I G H

Five large combine harvesters cross a Nebraska wheat field, gathering this grain crop. After corn, wheat is the most important grain crop produced in the United States.

In recent years annual snowfall in Lincoln has averaged about 26 inches (66 cm), creating work for adults but fun for kids.

SOUTH DAKOTA

Valentine
Niobrara
Fort Niobrara
National
Wildlife Refuge
Missouri
Lewis and
Clark Lake
SANTEE
INDIAN
RES.
Hartington
South
Sioux City
WINNEBAGO
I.R.
OMAHA
I.R.
IOWA

Gordon Cr.

Niobrara

Atkinson

Elkhorn

Logan Creek

H i l l s
Mullen
North Loup
Norfolk
Tekamah

Middle Loup
Burwell

E B R A S K A

Columbus
Fremont
Omaha

South Loup
Broken
Bow
Loup
Wahoo
Bellevue

North Platte
St. Paul
Big Blue
Plattsmouth

Platte
Gothenburg
Ravenna
Grand
Island
York
Platte

Red Willow Creek
Kearney
Hastings
★Lincoln
Crete
Nebraska
City

McCook
Holdrege
Minden
Geneva
Auburn
MISSOURI

Republican
Alma
Red Cloud
Little Blue
Fairbury
Big Nemaha
Missouri

Superior

SAC AND FOX I.R. IOWA
I.R.

KANSAS

Map Key

★ State capital
●●● City or town
■ Point of interest

⋯⋯ State boundary
▢ Indian Reservation
▢ National Forest land

N

0 ⸻⸻⸻ 50 miles
0 ⸻⸻⸻ 50 kilometers

Carhenge, near Alliance, is a sculpture made out of old cars that are painted gray and designed to look like Stonehenge, which is a famous archaeological site in southern England.

NORTH DAKOTA

LAND & WATER
The Badlands, the Red River of the North, and the Missouri River are important land and water features of North Dakota.

STATEHOOD
North Dakota became the 39th state in 1889.

PEOPLE & PLACES
North Dakota's population is 760,077. Bismarck is the state capital. The largest city is Fargo.

FUN FACT
North Dakota leads the United States in honey production, with more than 33 million pounds (14 million kg) produced annually. In addition to honey, bees produce wax and help pollinate crops.

North Dakota State Flag

Wild Prairie Rose
State Flower

Western Meadowlark
State Bird

Cowboys on the fence watch the excitement of the rodeo during the Slope County Fair in Amidon.

Fossils of prehistoric life, such as this leaf, can be found in North Dakota's sedimentary rock formations.

American bison are native to the Great Plains, but now they are found mainly in parks such as Sullys Hill National Game Preserve.

CANADA
U.S.

MONTANA

Missouri

Williston

Watford City

THEODORE ROOSEVELT N.P. (NORTH UNIT)

Yellowstone

Theodore Roosevelt N.P. (Elkhorn Ranch Site)

THEODORE ROOSEVELT N.P. (SOUTH UNIT)

Medora

Painted Canyon

Badlands

Amidon

White Butte
3,506 ft
1,069 m
Highest point in North Dakota

Little Missouri

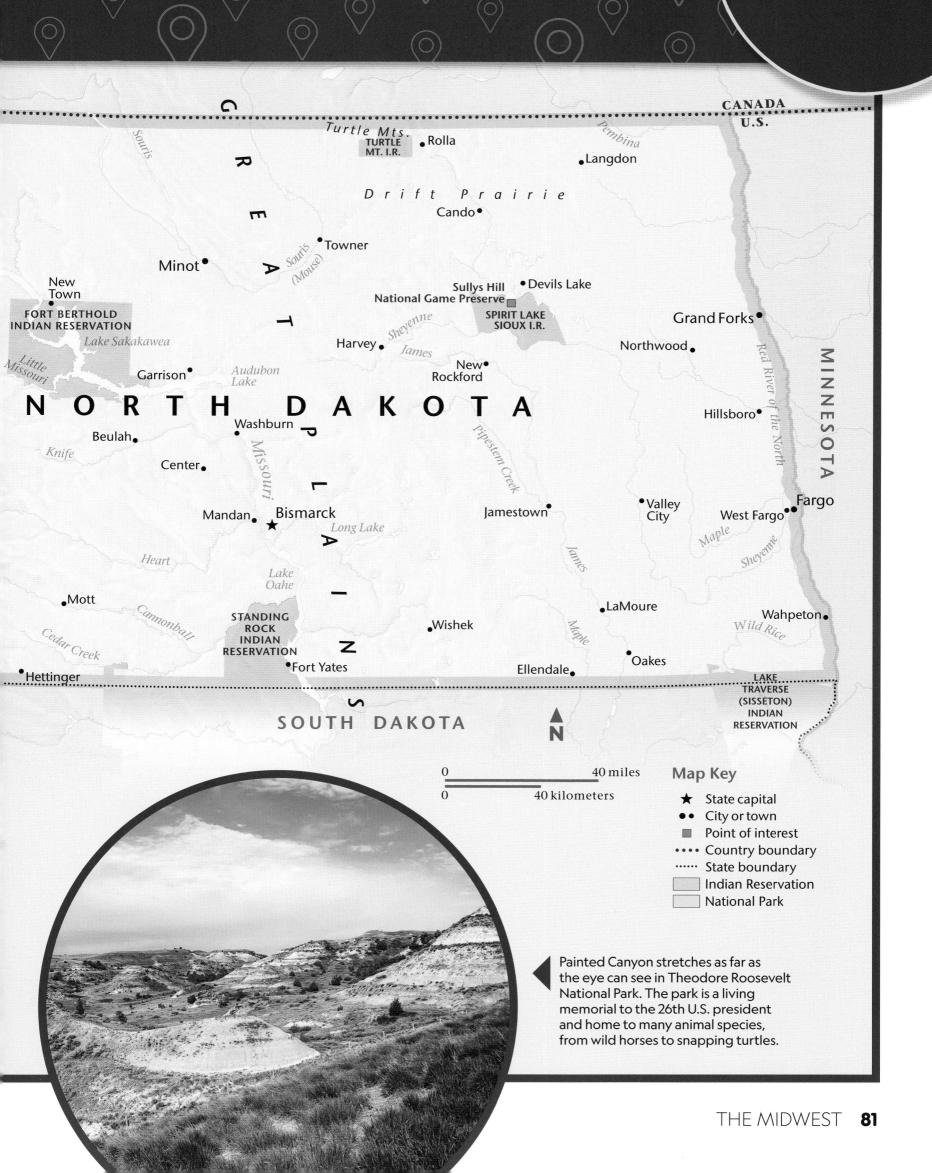

CANADA
U.S.

G R E A T

Turtle Mts.
TURTLE
MT. I.R.   •Rolla

•Langdon

D r i f t   P r a i r i e

Cando•

•Towner

Minot•

New
Town
FORT BERTHOLD
INDIAN RESERVATION

Souris

Souris (Mouse)

Sullys Hill
National Game Preserve   •Devils Lake

SPIRIT LAKE
SIOUX I.R.

Grand Forks•

Sheyenne

Harvey•   *James*   Northwood•

Lake Sakakawea

Little Missouri

Audubon Lake

Garrison•

New
Rockford•

Hillsboro•

N O R T H   D A K O T A

Washburn•

Beulah•

Knife

Center•

Missouri

P

L

A

Mandan•   Bismarck★

Long Lake

Jamestown•

Valley
City•

West Fargo•   Fargo•

Maple

Sheyenne

Heart

Lake Oahe

I

Pipestem Creek

James

•Mott

STANDING
ROCK
INDIAN
RESERVATION

Cannonball

•Wishek

LaMoure•

Wahpeton•

Maple

Wild Rice

Cedar Creek

N

•Hettinger   •Fort Yates

Ellendale•   •Oakes

LAKE
TRAVERSE
(SISSETON)
INDIAN
RESERVATION

S O U T H   D A K O T A

N

Red River of the North

M I N N E S O T A

0   40 miles
0   40 kilometers

Map Key

★ State capital
•• City or town
■ Point of interest
•••• Country boundary
······ State boundary
▇ Indian Reservation
▇ National Park

◀ Painted Canyon stretches as far as
the eye can see in Theodore Roosevelt
National Park. The park is a living
memorial to the 26th U.S. president
and home to many animal species,
from wild horses to snapping turtles.

OHIO

OHIO

LAND & WATER Wayne National Forest, Lake Erie, and the Ohio River are important land and water features of Ohio.

STATEHOOD Ohio became the 17th state in 1803.

PEOPLE & PLACES Ohio's population is 11,689,442. Columbus is the state capital and the largest city.

FUN FACT Ohio's nickname, the Buckeye State, comes from a local tree. The tree's name comes from Native Americans, who thought its seeds looked like the eye of a male deer, or buck.

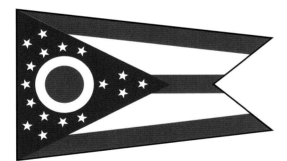

Ohio State Flag

Scarlet Carnation
State Flower

Cardinal
State Bird

Fourth of July fireworks light up the nighttime sky above Columbus. The city has been the state capital since 1816.

▲ Colorful guitars mark the entrance to the Rock and Roll Hall of Fame in downtown Cleveland.

The Blue Streak is the oldest operating roller coaster at Cedar Point Amusement Park in Sandusky. This popular ride is named after a local high school sports team.
▼

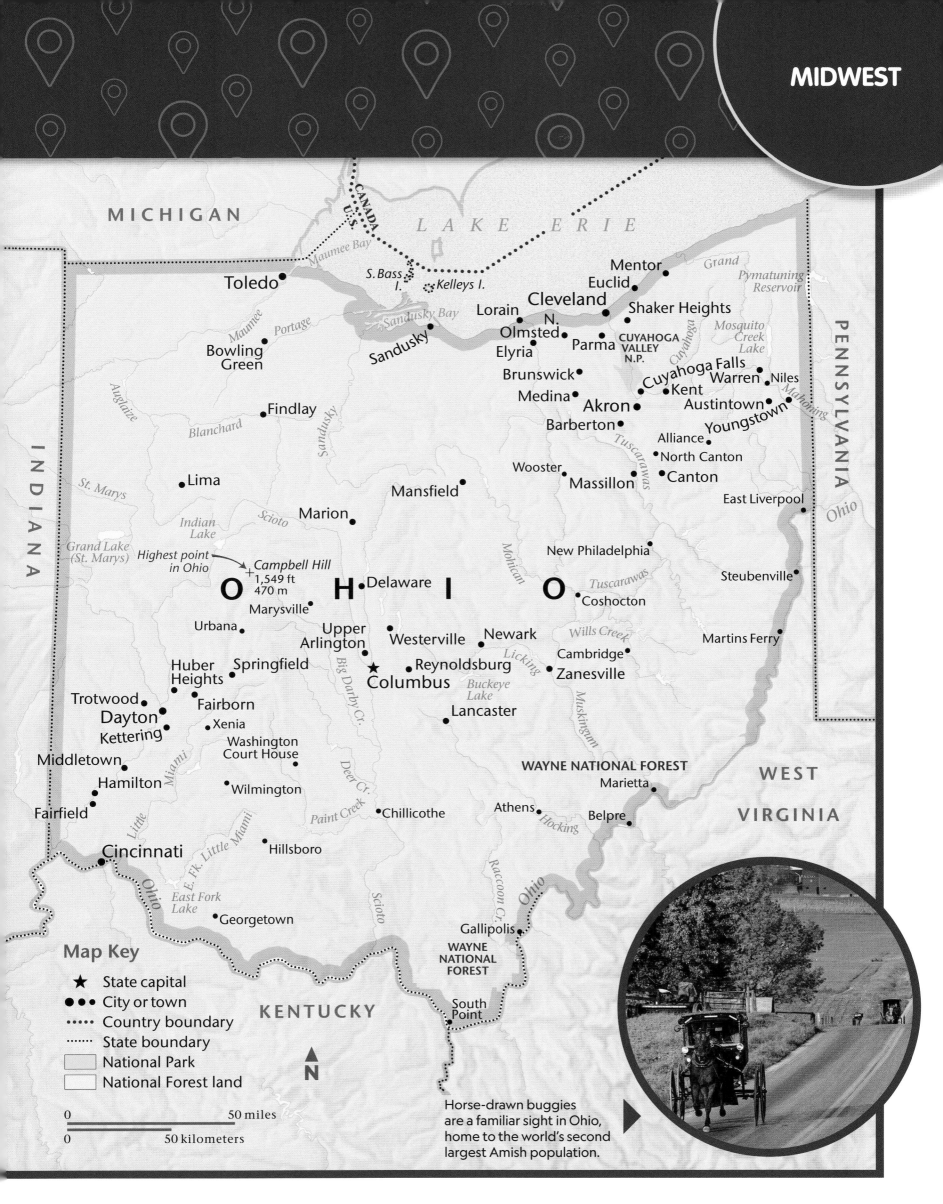

MICHIGAN

CANADA
U.S.

L A K E   E R I E

Maumee Bay

S. Bass I.

Kelleys I.

Toledo

Mentor

Euclid

Grand

Pymatuning
Reservoir

Cleveland

Lorain

Shaker Heights

N. Olmsted

Parma

CUYAHOGA
VALLEY
N.P.

Mosquito
Creek
Lake

Sandusky Bay

Elyria

Sandusky

Maumee

Portage

Bowling
Green

Brunswick

Cuyahoga Falls

Cuyahoga

Warren

Niles

Medina

Kent

Findlay

Blanchard

Sandusky

Akron

Austintown

Barberton

Youngstown

Mahoning

PENNSYLVANIA

Auglaize

Alliance

North Canton

Wooster

Massillon

Canton

Lima

Mansfield

East Liverpool

St. Marys

Marion

Scioto

Ohio

Indian
Lake

Grand Lake
(St. Marys)

Highest point
in Ohio

Campbell Hill
1,549 ft
470 m

New Philadelphia

Mohican

Steubenville

O H I O

Delaware

Tuscarawas

Marysville

Coshocton

Urbana

Upper
Arlington

Westerville

Newark

Wills Creek

Martins Ferry

Cambridge

Springfield

Reynoldsburg

Licking

Zanesville

Huber
Heights

Big Darby Cr.

Columbus

Buckeye
Lake

Fairborn

Muskingum

Trotwood

Xenia

Lancaster

Dayton

Kettering

Washington
Court House

Middletown

Deer Cr.

WAYNE NATIONAL FOREST

WEST

Hamilton

Miami

Wilmington

Marietta

Fairfield

Paint Creek

Chillicothe

Athens

Hocking

Belpre

VIRGINIA

Little Miami

Cincinnati

E. Fk. Little Miami

Hillsboro

Raccoon Cr.

Ohio

Ohio

East Fork
Lake

Georgetown

Scioto

Gallipolis

WAYNE
NATIONAL
FOREST

Map Key

★ State capital
●●● City or town
•••• Country boundary
⋯⋯ State boundary
☐ National Park
☐ National Forest land

KENTUCKY

South
Point

0   50 miles

0   50 kilometers

N

Horse-drawn buggies
are a familiar sight in Ohio,
home to the world's second
largest Amish population.

SOUTH DAKOTA

LAND & WATER The Black Hills, Badlands National Park, and the Missouri River are important land and water features of South Dakota.

STATEHOOD South Dakota became the 40th state in 1889.

PEOPLE & PLACES South Dakota's population is 882,235. Pierre is the state capital. The largest city is Sioux Falls.

FUN FACT A dinosaur nicknamed Sue was unearthed on the Cheyenne River Indian Reservation in 1990. It is the world's largest, most complete, and best preserved specimen of a *Tyrannosaurus rex*.

South Dakota State Flag

A mountain cottontail nibbles on some grass in Wind Cave National Park.

MONTANA

WYOMING

Little Missouri

• Buffalo

North Fork

South Fork

• Belle Fourche

• Sturgis
• Deadwood

Black Hills

Rapid City •

Black Elk Peak (Harney Peak) 7,242 ft 2,207 m
Mount Rushmore N.M.

Highest point in South Dakota

WIND CAVE N.P.

Hot Springs •

• Edgemont

Cheyenne

Carvings on Mount Rushmore in the Black Hills honor four past U.S. presidents (from left to right): George Washington, Thomas Jefferson, Theodore Roosevelt, and Abraham Lincoln.

Pasqueflower
State Flower

Ring-Necked Pheasant
State Bird

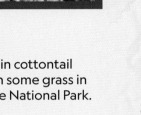

BEWARE
TYRANNOSAURUS
AHEAD

Widespread dinosaur fossils in South Dakota prompted this humorous sign.

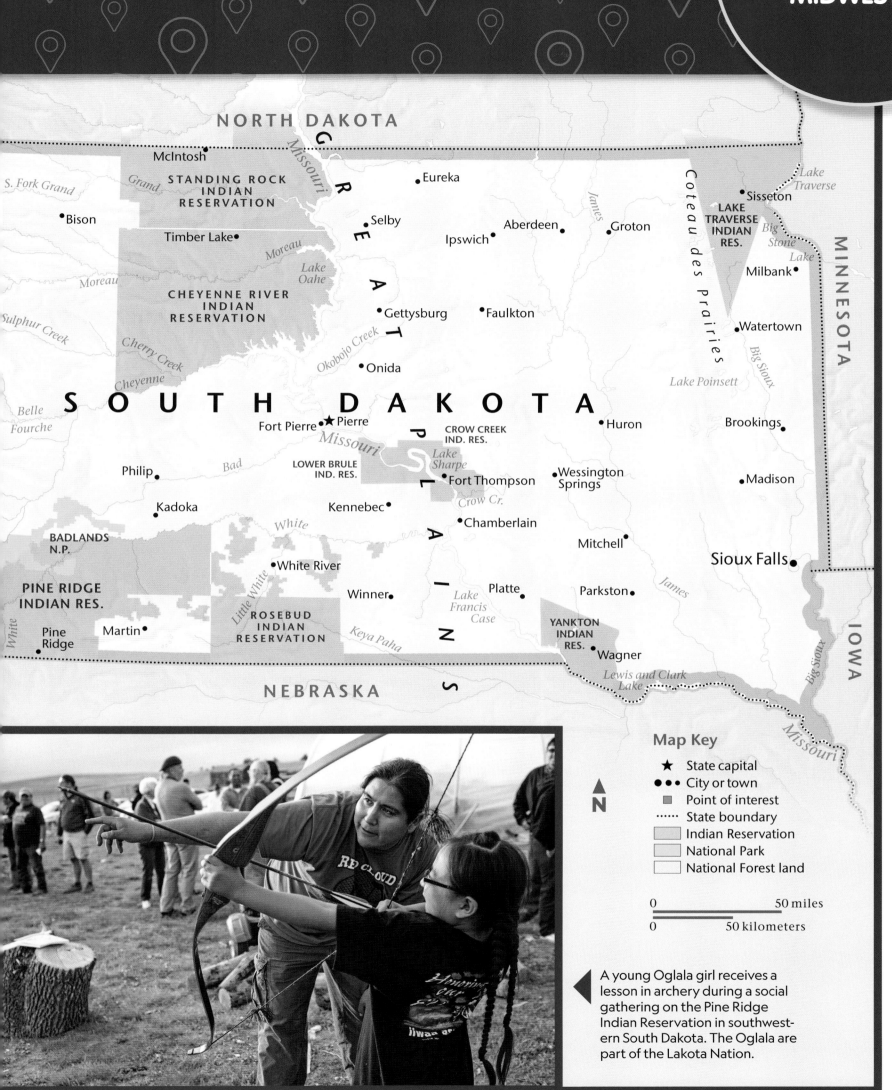

NORTH DAKOTA

McIntosh

STANDING ROCK INDIAN RESERVATION

Bison

Timber Lake

CHEYENNE RIVER INDIAN RESERVATION

S. Fork Grand

Grand

Moreau

Sulphur Creek

Cherry Creek

Cheyenne

Lake Oahe

Missouri

Eureka

Selby

Ipswich

Aberdeen

Groton

Gettysburg

Faulkton

Okobojo Creek

Onida

Coteau des prairies

Lake Traverse

Sisseton

LAKE TRAVERSE INDIAN RES.

Big Stone Lake

Milbank

Watertown

Lake Poinsett

Big Sioux

MINNESOTA

James

S O U T H   D A K O T A

Belle Fourche

Fort Pierre ★ Pierre

Missouri

Bad

CROW CREEK IND. RES.

LOWER BRULE IND. RES.

Lake Sharpe

Fort Thompson

Crow Cr.

Huron

Wessington Springs

Brookings

Madison

Philip

Kadoka

Kennebec

Chamberlain

White

Mitchell

Sioux Falls

BADLANDS N.P.

White

PINE RIDGE INDIAN RES.

White River

Little White

Winner

ROSEBUD INDIAN RESERVATION

Keya Paha

Lake Francis Case

Platte

Parkston

James

Pine Ridge

Martin

YANKTON INDIAN RES.

Wagner

Lewis and Clark Lake

Big Sioux

IOWA

Missouri

NEBRASKA

G R E A T   P L A I N S

Map Key

★ State capital
●●● City or town
■ Point of interest
••••• State boundary
▨ Indian Reservation
▨ National Park
□ National Forest land

N

0 ————————— 50 miles
0 ————————— 50 kilometers

◀ A young Oglala girl receives a lesson in archery during a social gathering on the Pine Ridge Indian Reservation in southwestern South Dakota. The Oglala are part of the Lakota Nation.

WISCONSIN

Bald eagles are found throughout Wisconsin. Almost 1,700 active nests were spotted in 2018.

LAND & WATER The Door Peninsula and Lakes Superior and Michigan are important land and water features of Wisconsin.

STATEHOOD
Wisconsin became the 30th state in 1848.

PEOPLE & PLACES Wisconsin's population is 5,813,568. Madison is the state capital. The largest city is Milwaukee.

FUN FACT Laura Ingalls Wilder was born in Pepin in 1867. Her famous Little House books are based on her childhood in the forests and prairies of the Midwest.

A Menominee boy works hard to control his rearing horse on the Menominee Indian Reservation near Keshena.

In a winter version of sailing, ice boats compete in a race on the frozen surface of Lake Winnebago near Oshkosh.

WISCONSIN

1848

Wisconsin State Flag

Robin
State Bird

Wood Violet
State Flower

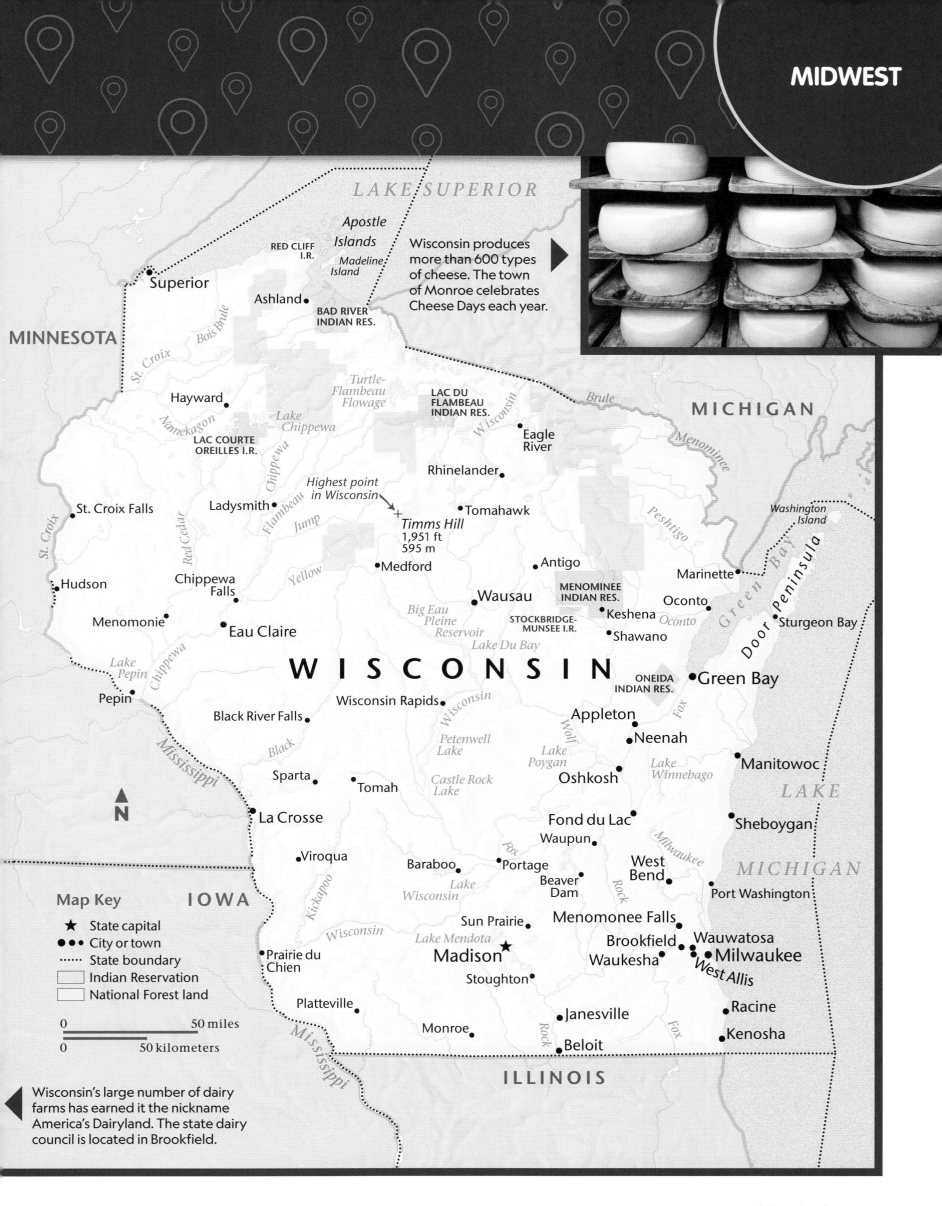

LAKE SUPERIOR

MINNESOTA

MICHIGAN

Apostle
Islands
RED CLIFF
I.R.
Madeline
Island

Superior

Ashland
BAD RIVER
INDIAN RES.

Wisconsin produces
more than 600 types
of cheese. The town
of Monroe celebrates
Cheese Days each year.

Bois Brule

St. Croix

Hayward

Namekagon

Lake
Chippewa

Turtle-
Flambeau
Flowage

LAC DU
FLAMBEAU
INDIAN RES.

Wisconsin

Brule

Eagle
River

LAC COURTE
OREILLES I.R.

Chippewa

Rhinelander

Menominee

St. Croix Falls

Ladysmith

Highest point
in Wisconsin

Tomahawk

Peshtigo

Washington
Island

St. Croix

Hudson

Chippewa
Falls

Flambeau

Jump

Timms Hill
1,951 ft
595 m

Medford

Antigo

Marinette

Oconto

Green Bay

Door Peninsula

Yellow

Red Cedar

Wausau

MENOMINEE
INDIAN RES.

Keshena

Oconto

Sturgeon Bay

Menomonie

Eau Claire

Big Eau
Pleine
Reservoir

STOCKBRIDGE-
MUNSEE I.R.

Shawano

Lake
Pepin

Chippewa

Lake Du Bay

WISCONSIN

ONEIDA
INDIAN RES.

Green Bay

Pepin

Wisconsin Rapids

Wisconsin

Appleton

Fox

Black River Falls

Black

Petenwell
Lake

Wolf

Neenah

Manitowoc

Sparta

Tomah

Castle Rock
Lake

Lake
Poygan

Oshkosh

Lake
Winnebago

LAKE

La Crosse

Mississippi

Fond du Lac

Sheboygan

Viroqua

Baraboo

Portage

Fox

Waupun

Milwaukee

MICHIGAN

IOWA

Kickapoo

Lake
Wisconsin

Beaver
Dam

Rock

West
Bend

Port Washington

Prairie du
Chien

Wisconsin

Sun Prairie

Lake Mendota

Menomonee Falls

Brookfield

Wauwatosa

Madison

Waukesha

Milwaukee

West Allis

Stoughton

Platteville

Monroe

Janesville

Rock

Racine

Kenosha

Beloit

Mississippi

ILLINOIS

Map Key

★ State capital

••• City or town

..... State boundary

[ ] Indian Reservation

[ ] National Forest land

0   50 miles
0   50 kilometers

N

Wisconsin's large number of dairy
farms has earned it the nickname
America's Dairyland. The state dairy
council is located in Brookfield.

THE SOUTHWEST

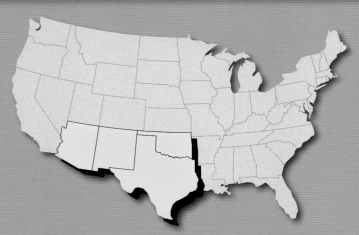

The Southwest region reaches from the Gulf Coast in the east to canyonlands in the west. Native Americans, descendants of early Spanish settlers, and recent immigrants from Mexico and Central America give this region a very diverse population. Agriculture, cattle ranching, and the oil industry are major economic activities. The Southwest's rapidly growing population is putting pressure on the region's water resources.

Wild horse herds are a common sight on open prairies and parklands of the Southwest. This horse roams free in Monument Valley, Arizona.

A rainbow frames Big Bend National Park's Cerro Castellon, in Texas. This eroded mount of volcanic rock rises almost 3,300 feet (1,006 m) above the desert floor.

ARIZONA

LAND & WATER The Colorado Plateau, the Grand Canyon, and the Colorado River are important land and water features of Arizona.

STATEHOOD Arizona became the 48th state in 1912.

PEOPLE & PLACES Arizona's population is 7,171,646. Phoenix is the state capital and the largest city.

FUN FACT Of the 21 Native American reservations in Arizona, the largest belongs to the Navajo Nation. Native peoples and the federal government own almost 70 percent of the state's land area.

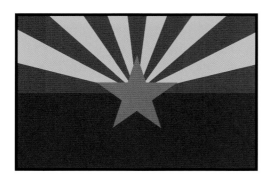

Arizona State Flag

Cactus Wren
State Bird

Saguaro
State Flower

Daring boaters get soaked as they run the rapids on the fast-flowing waters of the Colorado River in Grand Canyon National Park.

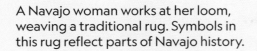

Saguaro cactus, found in the Sonoran Desert, can grow more than 30 feet (9 m) tall.

A Navajo woman works at her loom, weaving a traditional rug. Symbols in this rug reflect parts of Navajo history.

UTAH

COLORADO

NEVADA

Only spot in the U.S. where the borders of four states come together

Colorado

Lake Powell

FOUR CORNERS

KAIBAB I.R.

• Page

C O L O R A D O

NAVAJO NATION INDIAN RESERVATION

GRAND CANYON NATIONAL PARK

Lake Mead

Grand Canyon

HAVASUPAI I.R.

• Grand Canyon

HOPI I.R.

HOPI INDIAN RESERVATION

Colorado

Fort Defiance •

P L A T E A U

HUALAPAI I.R.

FT. MOJAVE I.R.

• Kingman

Humphreys Peak ✛
12,633 ft
3,851 m

Highest point in Arizona

• Flagstaff

PETRIFIED FOREST N.P.

Holbrook •

NEW MEXICO

YAVAPAI-PRESCOTT I.R.

YAVAPAI-APACHE I.R.

ZUNI I.R.

Little Colorado

Prescott •

A R I Z O N A

TONTO APACHE I.R.

WHITE MOUNTAIN APACHE INDIAN RESERVATION

CALIFORNIA

Colorado

COLORADO RIVER INDIAN RESERVATION

Sun City •

SALT RIVER I.R.

FT. McDOWELL I.R.

SAN CARLOS APACHE INDIAN RESERVATION

• Quartzsite

Glendale •

★ Scottsdale

Phoenix • Mesa

Globe •

Tempe • • Chandler

Gila

S O N O R A N

Gila

GILA RIVER INDIAN RES.

MARICOPA (AK-CHIN) I.R.

TOHONO O'ODHAM I.R.

Casa Grande •

• Safford

Gila

FORT YUMA I.R.

D E S E R T

Yuma

COCOPAH I.R.

Ajo •

SAGUARO NAT. PARK

Colorado

TOHONO O'ODHAM INDIAN RESERVATION

PASCUA YAQUI I.R.

Tucson •

SAGUARO NAT. PARK

Willcox Playa

TOHONO O'ODHAM I.R.

• Tombstone

U.S. MEXICO

U.S. MEXICO

Nogales •

Gulf of California

Map Key

★ State capital
• • • City or town
■ Point of interest
• • • • Country boundary
• • • • • State boundary

▦ Dry lake
▢ Indian Reservation
National Park
National Forest land

N

0 ——— 50 miles
0 ——— 50 kilometers

NEW MEXICO

 LAND & WATER The Sangre de Cristo Mountains, Carlsbad Caverns, and the Rio Grande are important land and water features of New Mexico.

 STATEHOOD New Mexico became the 47th state in 1912.

 PEOPLE & PLACES New Mexico's population is 2,095,428. Santa Fe is the state capital. The largest city is Albuquerque.

FUN FACT Roswell attracts people interested in unidentified flying objects (UFOs). A rancher discovered what he believed to be wreckage of one in 1947.

Brightly colored hot-air balloons rise into a blue sky above Albuquerque during the International Balloon Fiesta, the largest such event in the world.

New Mexico State Flag

One of the world's oldest cave systems, Carlsbad Caverns, lies beneath the Guadalupe Mountains. The caverns include more than 119 chambers of all sizes.

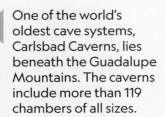

Chili peppers, seen here in a store in Santa Fe, give Southwestern food a spicy taste. New Mexico is second only to California in the production of chilies.

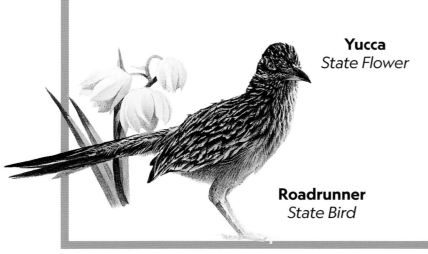

Yucca
State Flower

Roadrunner
State Bird

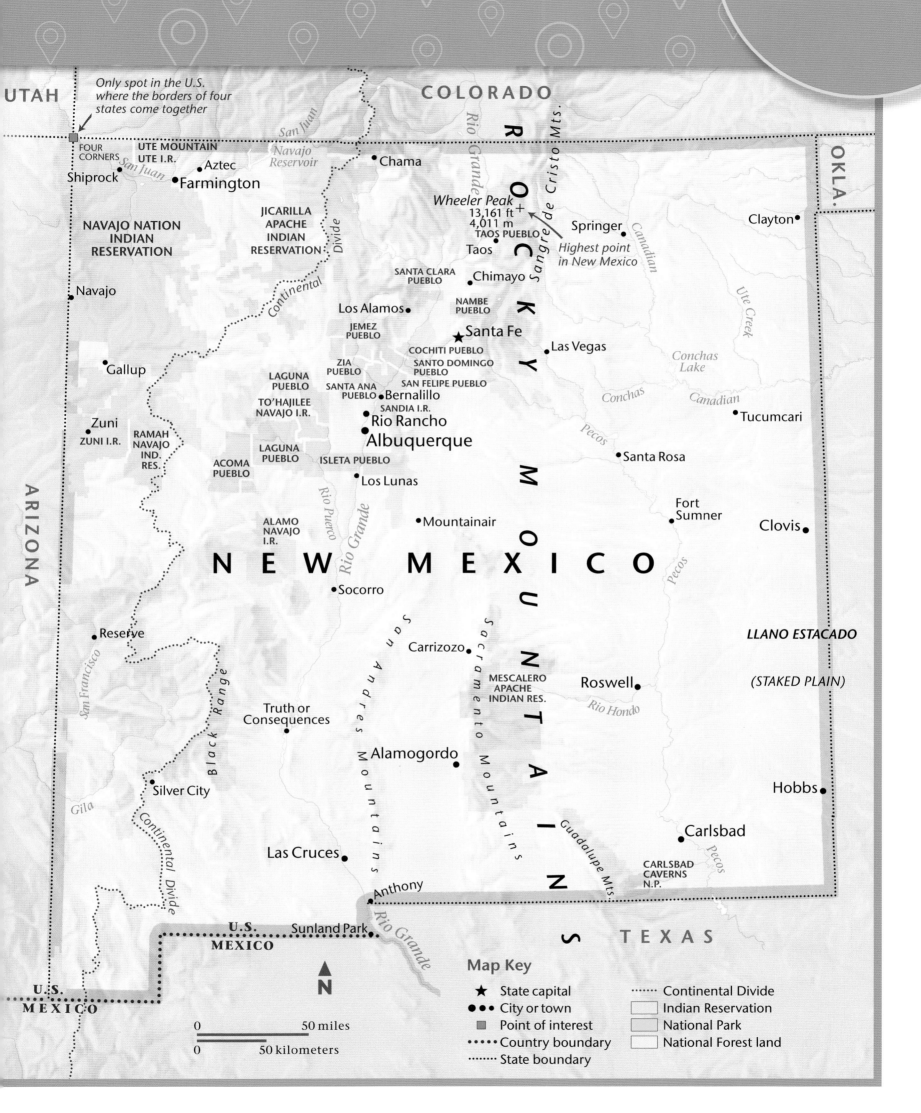

UTAH

COLORADO

OKLA.

Only spot in the U.S. where the borders of four states come together

FOUR CORNERS

UTE MOUNTAIN UTE I.R.

Shiprock

San Juan

Aztec

Farmington

Navajo Reservoir

Chama

San Juan

Rio Grande

R O C K Y

Sangre de Cristo Mts.

Wheeler Peak
13,161 ft +
4,011 m

Springer

Clayton

NAVAJO NATION INDIAN RESERVATION

JICARILLA APACHE INDIAN RESERVATION

Continental Divide

TAOS PUEBLO

Taos

Highest point in New Mexico

Canadian

Navajo

SANTA CLARA PUEBLO

Chimayo

Ute Creek

Los Alamos

NAMBE PUEBLO

Gallup

JEMEZ PUEBLO

Santa Fe

Las Vegas

Conchas Lake

ZIA PUEBLO

COCHITI PUEBLO

SANTO DOMINGO PUEBLO

Conchas

Canadian

Zuni

ZUNI I.R.

LAGUNA PUEBLO

SANTA ANA PUEBLO

SAN FELIPE PUEBLO

Pecos

Tucumcari

RAMAH NAVAJO IND. RES.

TO'HAJILEE NAVAJO I.R.

Bernalillo

SANDIA I.R.

Rio Rancho

Albuquerque

Santa Rosa

ACOMA PUEBLO

LAGUNA PUEBLO

ISLETA PUEBLO

Los Lunas

K

Y

Fort Sumner

Clovis

ALAMO NAVAJO I.R.

Rio Puerco

Rio Grande

Mountainair

M O U N T A I N S

N E W   M E X I C O

LLANO ESTACADO

Reserve

Socorro

Pecos

(STAKED PLAIN)

San Francisco

Black Range

San Andres Mountains

Carrizozo

Sacramento Mountains

MESCALERO APACHE INDIAN RES.

Roswell

Rio Hondo

Truth or Consequences

Silver City

Continental Divide

Alamogordo

Guadalupe Mts.

Carlsbad

Hobbs

Gila

Las Cruces

Anthony

Pecos

CARLSBAD CAVERNS N.P.

ARIZONA

U.S.
MEXICO

Sunland Park

Rio Grande

TEXAS

U.S.
MEXICO

Map Key

★ State capital

● ● ● City or town

■ Point of interest

••••• Country boundary

••••• State boundary

••••• Continental Divide

▭ Indian Reservation

▭ National Park

▭ National Forest land

N

| 0 | 50 miles |
| 0 | 50 kilometers |

OKLAHOMA

 LAND & WATER Black Mesa, the Ouachita Mountains, and the Arkansas River are important land and water features of Oklahoma.

 STATEHOOD Oklahoma became the 46th state in 1907.

 PEOPLE & PLACES Oklahoma's population is 3,943,079. Oklahoma City is the state capital and the largest city.

 FUN FACT Before it became a state, Oklahoma was known as Indian Territory. Today 39 nations, including the Cherokee, Creek, Osage, and Choctaw, have their headquarters in the state.

Oklahoma State Flag

Scissor-Tailed Flycatcher
State Bird

Rose
State Flower

COLORADO

NEW MEXICO

Cimarron

Black Mesa
4,973 ft
1,516 m

← Boise City

Highest point in Oklahoma

H I G H

Beaver
Beaver

Optima Lake

P L A I N S

A tornado is a destructive rotating column of air that forms from a thunderstorm. In 1974 five tornadoes struck Oklahoma City in one day.

The collared lizard is Oklahoma's state reptile. The lizard is common in the Wichita Mountains and throughout the state.

KANSAS

MISSOURI

Buffalo

Great
Salt Plains
Lake

Kaw
Lake

OSAGE NATION
INDIAN RES.

Miami

Lake O' The
Cherokees

Salt Fork

Pawhuska

Bartlesville

Vinita

Ponca
City

Arkansas

Verdigris

Woodward

Rock Creek

Oologah
Lake

Fairview

Enid

Sooner
Lake

Skiatook
Lake

Pryor

Lake
Hudson

North Canadian

Owasso

Cimarron

Keystone
Lake

Tulsa

Ft. Gibson
Lake

Stillwater

Broken
Arrow

Illinois

Canadian

Bixby

Tahlequah

OZARK PLATEAU

O K L A H O M A

Muskogee

Edmond

Okmulgee

Tenkiller
Lake

ARKANSAS

El Reno

Oklahoma City

Deep Fork

Sallisaw

Clinton

Arkansas

Moore

Shawnee

N. Canadian

Robert
S. Kerr
Lake

Sayre

Washita

Norman

Little

Seminole

Eufaula
Lake

Poteau

North Fork

Chickasha

Canadian

Elm Fork

Hobart

Anadarko

McAlester

Heavener

Mangum

Purcell

Sardis
Lake

Ouachita Mountains

Wichita Mts.

Pauls Valley

Ada

Hollis

Salt Fork

Lawton

Washita

Sulphur

McGee Cr.
Lake

Kiamichi

Atoka

Prairie Dog Town Fork

Duncan

Frederick

Arbuckle Mts.

Broken Bow
Lake

Walters

Red

Ardmore

Hugo

Hugo
Lake

Lake
Texoma

Durant

Idabel

TEXAS

Red

Red

Map Key

★ State capital
●●● City or town
⋯⋯ State boundary
▢ Indian Reservation
▢ National Forest land

N

| 0 | | 50 miles |
| 0 | 50 kilometers | |

A young Osage boy wearing ceremonial dress reflects the strong Native American heritage in Oklahoma.

The Golden Driller, with his hand on an oil rig, stands 76 feet (23 m) tall near the State Fairgrounds in Tulsa.

TULSA

TEXAS

TEXAS

 LAND & WATER The Edwards Plateau, Padre Island National Seashore, and the Rio Grande are important land and water features of Texas.

 STATEHOOD Texas became the 28th state in 1845.

PEOPLE & PLACES The population of Texas is 28,701,845. Austin is the state capital. Houston is the largest city.

FUN FACT The Texas Rangers, the country's oldest state law enforcement organization, was established in 1823 to protect settlements in the territory that would become Texas.

Texas State Flag

The brightly lit Congress Avenue Bridge crosses Town Lake into downtown Austin, where tall buildings rise against the night sky.

Texas leads the United States in oil and natural gas production. A well near Houston pumps oil, called "black gold" because it's worth so much money.

NEW MEXICO

GUADALUPE MTS. N.P.

El Paso

+Guadalupe Peak 8,751 ft 2,667 m

Highest point in Texas

U.S.

MEXICO

Rio Grande

Davis Mts

Presidio

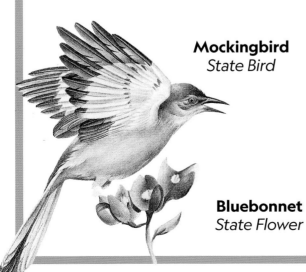

Mockingbird
State Bird

The colorful coachwhip snake is found in western Texas. It can grow up to six feet (1.8 m) long.

Bluebonnet
State Flower

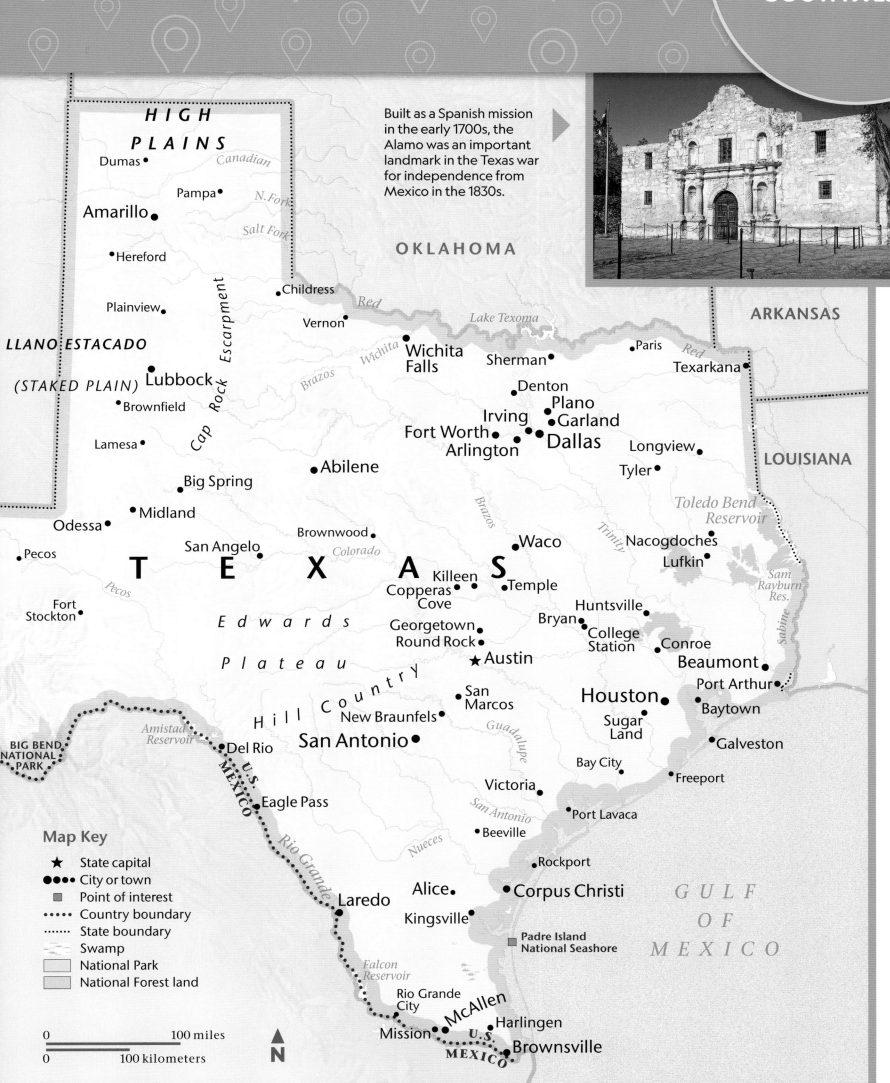

HIGH PLAINS

Dumas

Pampa

Amarillo

Canadian

N. Fork

Salt Fork

Hereford

OKLAHOMA

Built as a Spanish mission in the early 1700s, the Alamo was an important landmark in the Texas war for independence from Mexico in the 1830s.

Plainview

LLANO ESTACADO

(STAKED PLAIN)

Childress

Red

Lake Texoma

Vernon

Wichita Falls

Sherman

Paris

ARKANSAS

Red

Texarkana

Cap Rock Escarpment

Wichita

Brazos

Denton

Plano

Lubbock

Brownfield

Irving

Garland

LOUISIANA

Fort Worth

Dallas

Lamesa

Arlington

Longview

Abilene

Tyler

Toledo Bend Reservoir

Big Spring

Brazos

Waco

Nacogdoches

Midland

Brownwood

Lufkin

Odessa

Colorado

Trinity

Sam Rayburn Res.

Pecos

San Angelo

T   E   X   A   S

Killeen

Temple

Fort Stockton

Pecos

Copperas Cove

Huntsville

College Station

Bryan

Conroe

Sabine

Edwards

Georgetown

Round Rock

Beaumont

Plateau

★ Austin

Port Arthur

Hill Country

San Marcos

Houston

Baytown

New Braunfels

Sugar Land

BIG BEND NATIONAL PARK

Amistad Reservoir

Del Rio

San Antonio

Guadalupe

Bay City

Galveston

Freeport

Eagle Pass

San Antonio

Victoria

Port Lavaca

U.S.

MEXICO

Nueces

Beeville

Rio Grande

Rockport

Map Key

★ State capital

●●●● City or town

■ Point of interest

•••• Country boundary

···· State boundary

Swamp

National Park

National Forest land

Alice

Corpus Christi

GULF

OF

MEXICO

Laredo

Kingsville

Falcon Reservoir

Padre Island National Seashore

Rio Grande City

McAllen

Harlingen

0   100 miles

0   100 kilometers

N

Mission

U.S.

MEXICO

Brownsville

THE WEST

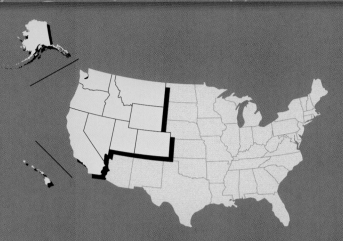

The West region makes up almost half the landmass of the United States. The region's varied landscapes range from the frozen heights of Denali in Alaska to the barren desert of Death Valley in California and the lush tropical forests of Hawai'i. More than half the population lives in California, where Los Angeles ranks second only to New York City in number of people. Other parts of the West have few people. Much of the region's land is set aside as parkland and military bases.

Bobcats, named for their short tail, have adapted to environments ranging from forests to deserts and snow-covered mountains.

The snowy peaks of Maroon Bells–Snowmass Wilderness near Aspen, Colorado, rise over 14,000 feet (4,200 m). Mountains—including the Rockies, Tetons, and Sierra Nevada—are important landscape features of the West.

ALASKA

ALASKA

LAND & WATER The Tongass National Forest, Brooks Range, and the Yukon River are important land and water features of Alaska.

STATEHOOD Alaska became the 49th state in 1959.

PEOPLE & PLACES Alaska's population is 737,438. Juneau is the state capital. The largest city is Anchorage.

FUN FACT The most powerful earthquake ever recorded in North America struck Anchorage in 1964. Eighty times more powerful than the 1906 San Francisco earthquake, it measured 9.2 on the Richter scale.

Dogsledding has a long and colorful history in Alaska. The most famous race is the Iditarod, which follows an old mail and supply route from Anchorage to Nome.

CHUKCHI

ASIA

Bering

St. Lawrence I.

St. Matthew I.

Nunivak I.

BERING SEA

St. Paul • Pribilof Islands

Alaska State Flag

Forget-Me-Not
State Flower

Willow Ptarmigan
State Bird

ALEUTIAN ISLANDS
Unimak I.
Unalaska I.
Umnak I. • Unalaska
Yunaska I. Islands of Four Mountains

Continuation of the Aleutian Islands on map to the right

PACIFIC OCEAN

Native peoples in Alaska carve totem poles to tell their histories. One place carvers still make totems is Saxman Native Village in Ketchikan.

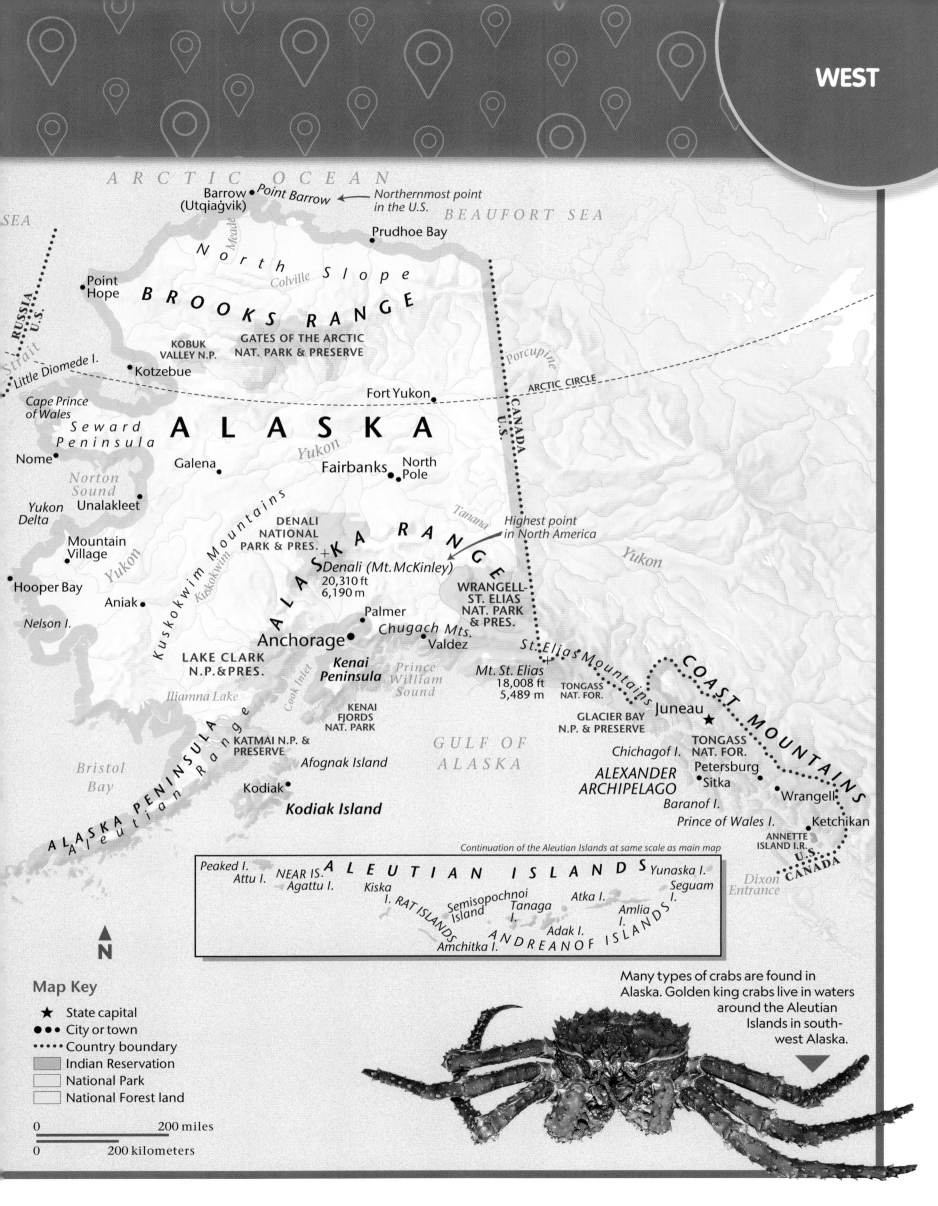

A R C T I C   O C E A N

Barrow • Point Barrow ← Northernmost point
(Utqiaġvik) in the U.S.

SEA *BEAUFORT SEA*

• Prudhoe Bay

Meade

North   Slope

Colville

Point
Hope •

B R O O K S   R A N G E

KOBUK
VALLEY N.P.

GATES OF THE ARCTIC
NAT. PARK & PRESERVE

Porcupine

RUSSIA
U.S.
Strait

• Little Diomede I.

• Kotzebue

ARCTIC CIRCLE

Cape Prince
of Wales

*S e w a r d
P e n i n s u l a*

Fort Yukon •

CANADA
U.S.

Nome •

Galena •

A L A S K A

Yukon

Fairbanks • North
Pole •

*Norton
Sound*

Unalakleet •

*Yukon
Delta*

Mountain
Village •

Yukon

Kuskokwim Mountains

DENALI
NATIONAL
PARK & PRES.

A L A S K A   R A N G E

Tanana

Highest point
in North America

Yukon

Hooper Bay •

Aniak •

Kuskokwim

+
Denali (Mt. McKinley)
20,310 ft
6,190 m

WRANGELL-
ST. ELIAS
NAT. PARK
& PRES.

Nelson I.

Palmer •

Chugach Mts.

Anchorage •

Valdez •

St. Elias Mountains

C O A S T   M O U N T A I N S

LAKE CLARK
N.P. & PRES.

*Kenai
Peninsula*

*Prince
William
Sound*

Mt. St. Elias
18,008 ft
5,489 m

TONGASS
NAT. FOR.

Cook Inlet

Iliamna Lake

KENAI
FJORDS
NAT. PARK

GLACIER BAY
N.P. & PRESERVE

Juneau ★

A L A S K A   P E N I N S U L A

Aleutian Range

KATMAI N.P. &
PRESERVE

Afognak Island

*GULF OF
ALASKA*

Chichagof I.

TONGASS
NAT. FOR.

Petersburg •

*Bristol
Bay*

Kodiak •

**ALEXANDER
ARCHIPELAGO**

• Sitka

• Wrangell

Baranof I.

Prince of Wales I.

• Ketchikan

Kodiak Island

ANNETTE
ISLAND I.R.

U.S.
CANADA

Continuation of the Aleutian Islands at same scale as main map

Peaked I.
Attu I.

NEAR IS.

A L E U T I A N   I S L A N D S

Yunaska I.

*Dixon
Entrance*

Agattu I.

Kiska

Seguam

I. RAT ISLANDS

*Semisopochnoi
Island*

*Tanaga
I.*

Atka I.

*Amlia
I.*

I.

Adak I.

A N D R E A N O F   I S L A N D S

Amchitka I.

N

Map Key

★ State capital
●●● City or town
····· Country boundary
▨ Indian Reservation
☐ National Park
☐ National Forest land

0 — 200 miles
0 — 200 kilometers

Many types of crabs are found in
Alaska. Golden king crabs live in waters
around the Aleutian
Islands in south-
west Alaska.

▼

CALIFORNIA

Stretching more than a mile (1.6 km) across the entrance to San Francisco Bay, the Golden Gate Bridge opened in 1937.

 LAND & WATER The Sierra Nevada, Death Valley, and San Francisco Bay are important land and water features of California.

 STATEHOOD California became the 31st state in 1850.

 PEOPLE & PLACES California's population is 39,557,045. Sacramento is the state capital. The largest city is Los Angeles.

 FUN FACT In July 1913, what is now Furnace Creek Ranch in Death Valley experienced a temperature of 134°F (57°C)— the highest temperature ever recorded in the United States.

CALIFORNIA REPUBLIC

California State Flag

On a beach near San Simeon two bull elephant seals face off in a loud roaring match in front of sleeping females and pups.

The Tour Thru Tree, near Klamath, is 800 years old and 168 feet (51 m) tall. A tunnel carved through the trunk allows cars to drive through.

Golden Poppy
State Flower

California Quail
State Bird

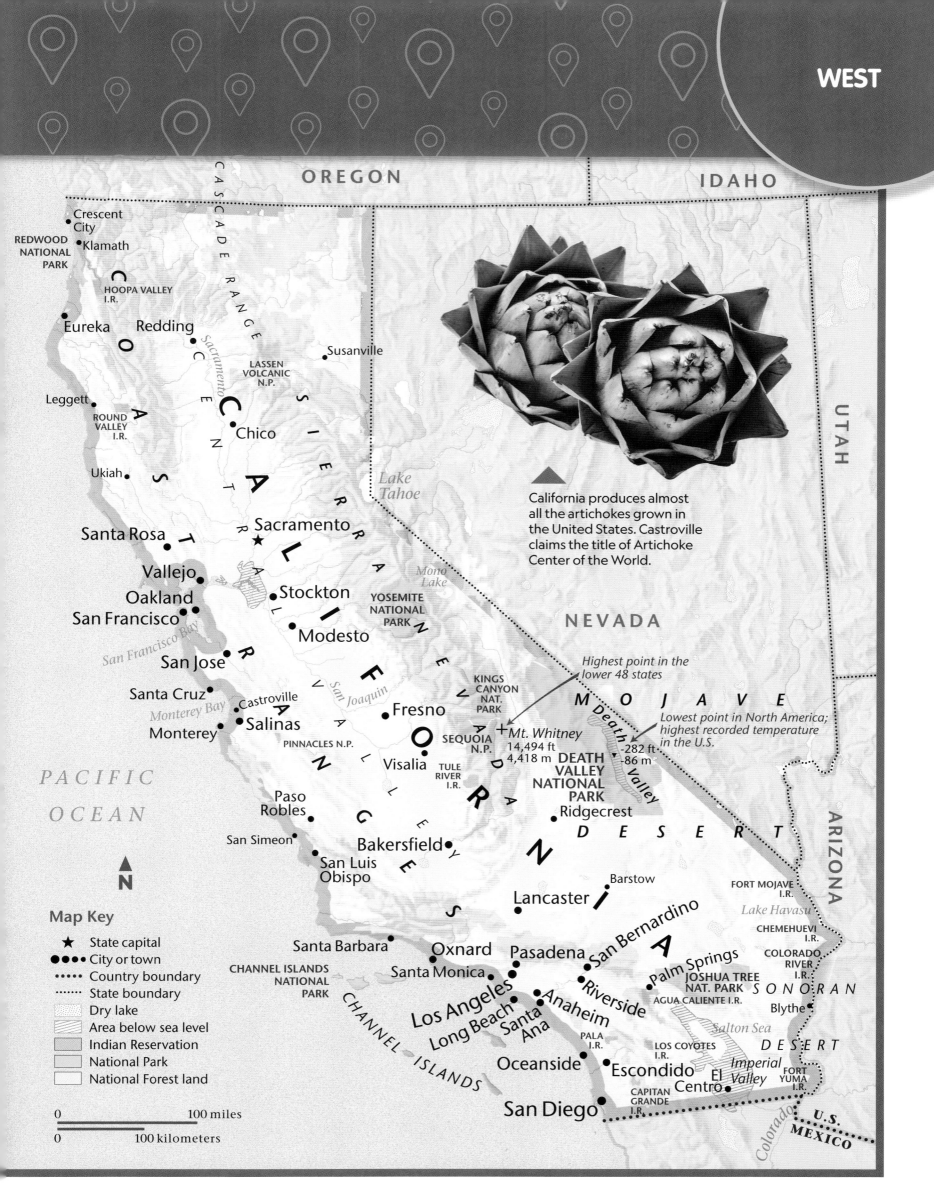

OREGON

IDAHO

UTAH

NEVADA

ARIZONA

Crescent City
Klamath
REDWOOD NATIONAL PARK
HOOPA VALLEY I.R.
Eureka
Redding
Susanville
LASSEN VOLCANIC N.P.
Leggett
ROUND VALLEY I.R.
Chico
Ukiah
CASCADE RANGE
SIERRA
Lake Tahoe
Santa Rosa
Sacramento
Mono Lake
Vallejo
Stockton
YOSEMITE NATIONAL PARK
Oakland
San Francisco
Modesto
San Francisco Bay
San Jose
Santa Cruz
Castroville
Monterey Bay
Salinas
San Joaquin
Fresno
KINGS CANYON NAT. PARK
Monterey
PINNACLES N.P.
SEQUOIA N.P.
Mt. Whitney 14,494 ft 4,418 m
Highest point in the lower 48 states
DEATH VALLEY NATIONAL PARK
Death Valley
-282 ft -86 m
Lowest point in North America; highest recorded temperature in the U.S.

California produces almost all the artichokes grown in the United States. Castroville claims the title of Artichoke Center of the World.

Visalia
TULE RIVER I.R.
Ridgecrest
DESERT
PACIFIC OCEAN
Paso Robles
San Simeon
Bakersfield
San Luis Obispo
Barstow
Lancaster
FORT MOJAVE I.R.
Lake Havasu
MOJAVE
CHEMEHUEVI I.R.
Santa Barbara
Oxnard
Pasadena
San Bernardino
Palm Springs
COLORADO RIVER I.R.
Santa Monica
JOSHUA TREE NAT. PARK
SONORAN
Riverside
AGUA CALIENTE I.R.
Blythe
Los Angeles
Anaheim
Long Beach
Santa Ana
PALA I.R.
LOS COYOTES I.R.
Salton Sea
DESERT
CHANNEL ISLANDS NATIONAL PARK
Oceanside
Escondido
El Centro
Imperial Valley
FORT YUMA I.R.
CHANNEL ISLANDS
CAPITAN GRANDE I.R.
San Diego
Colorado
U.S.
MEXICO

Map Key

★ State capital
●●●● City or town
···· Country boundary
······ State boundary
Dry lake
Area below sea level
Indian Reservation
National Park
National Forest land

N

0   100 miles
0   100 kilometers

COLORADO

COLORADO

LAND & WATER The Rocky Mountains, Mount Elbert, and the Colorado River are important land and water features of Colorado.

STATEHOOD Colorado became the 38th state in 1876.

PEOPLE & PLACES Colorado's population is 5,695,564. Denver is the state capital and the largest city.

FUN FACT The 700-foot (210-m)-high sand dunes in Great Sand Dunes National Park and Preserve occupy an area that was covered by an ancient sea more than a million years ago.

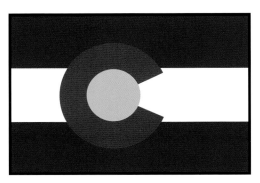
Colorado State Flag

Early native people built more than 600 stone structures into cliff walls that are now part of Mesa Verde National Park.

Bighorn sheep, known for their large curled horns, live in Rocky Mountain National Park and other mountainous areas of the West.

Columbine
State Flower

Lark Bunting
State Bird

Rangely
Danforth
White
Cathedral Bluffs
Roan Plateau
Grand Valley
Grand Junction
Grand
UTAH
Colorado
Dolores
Uncompahgre
San Miguel
Cortez
MESA VERDE N.P.
UTE MOUNTAIN I.R.
Four Corners
San Juan
Mancos
ARIZONA
Only spot in the U.S. where the borders of four states come together

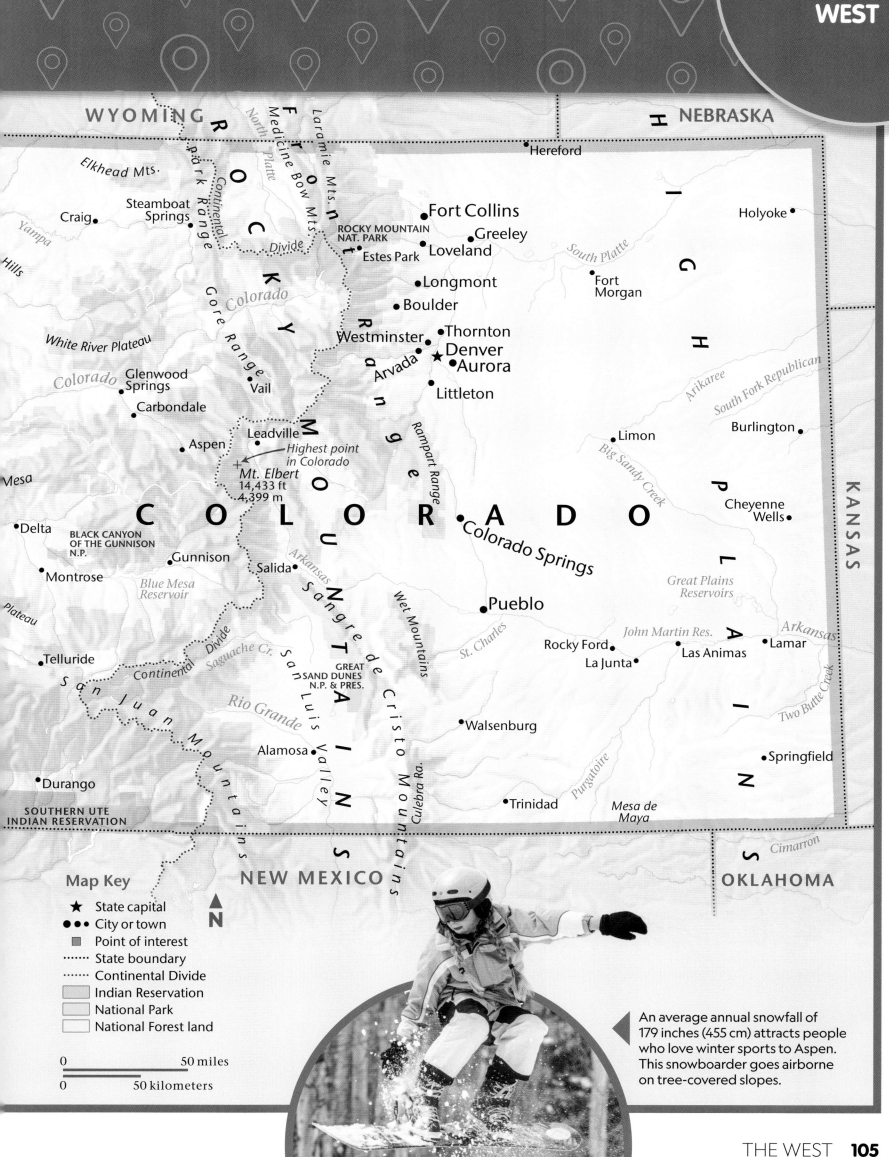

WYOMING

NEBRASKA

Elkhead Mts.

Craig

Steamboat Springs

Yampa

Hills

ROCKY MOUNTAIN NAT. PARK

Hereford

Holyoke

Fort Collins

Greeley

Estes Park

Loveland

Longmont

Fort Morgan

White River Plateau

Colorado

Boulder

Westminster

Thornton

Denver

Arvada

Aurora

South Platte

Glenwood Springs

Vail

Littleton

Carbondale

Arikaree

South Fork Republican

Leadville

Aspen

Highest point in Colorado

Limon

Burlington

Big Sandy Creek

+ Mt. Elbert
14,433 ft
4,399 m

Mesa

Delta

BLACK CANYON OF THE GUNNISON N.P.

C O L O R A D O

Cheyenne Wells

Montrose

Gunnison

Salida

Blue Mesa Reservoir

Colorado Springs

Great Plains Reservoirs

Plateau

Telluride

Pueblo

Arkansas

St. Charles

Rocky Ford

La Junta

John Martin Res.

Las Animas

Lamar

GREAT SAND DUNES N.P. & PRES.

Rio Grande

Alamosa

Walsenburg

Springfield

Durango

SOUTHERN UTE INDIAN RESERVATION

Trinidad

Mesa de Maya

Purgatoire

Two Butte Creek

NEW MEXICO

OKLAHOMA

Cimarron

Map Key

★ State capital
●● City or town
■ Point of interest
.... State boundary
.... Continental Divide
▧ Indian Reservation
▧ National Park
▢ National Forest land

N

0 _____ 50 miles
0 _____ 50 kilometers

An average annual snowfall of 179 inches (455 cm) attracts people who love winter sports to Aspen. This snowboarder goes airborne on tree-covered slopes.

HAWAI'I

HAWAI'I

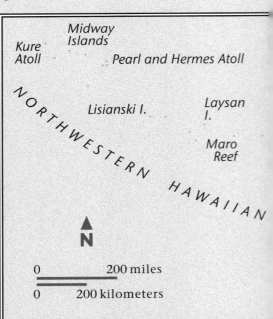

LAND & WATER Kilauea crater, Diamond Head, and Pearl Harbor are important land and water features of Hawai'i.

STATEHOOD
Hawai'i became the 50th state in 1959.

PEOPLE & PLACES
Hawai'i's population is 1,420,491. Honolulu is the state capital and the largest city.

FUN FACT Hawai'i is the fastest growing state in the United States—not in people, but in land. Each of the islands that make up the state was created by lava from erupting volcanoes.

Hawai'i State Flag

Hibiscus
State Flower

Hawaiian Goose (Nene)
State Bird

Recent eruptions on Kilauea, Hawai'i's most active volcano, have added almost 900 acres (364 ha) of new land to the state.

KAUA'I

Lehua

Kaulakahi Channel

Waimea Canyon

Wai'ale'ale
5,148 ft
1,569 m

Kekaha

Kapa'a

Lihu'e

Kalaheo

Pu'uwai

NI'IHAU

Kaua'i

PACIFIC

A lei, or necklace made of flowers such as orchids, is the traditional gift of greeting or farewell in Hawai'i.

Kure Atoll

Midway Islands

Pearl and Hermes Atoll

Lisianski I.

Laysan I.

Maro Reef

NORTHWESTERN HAWAIIAN

N

| 0 | 200 miles |
| 0 | 200 kilometers |

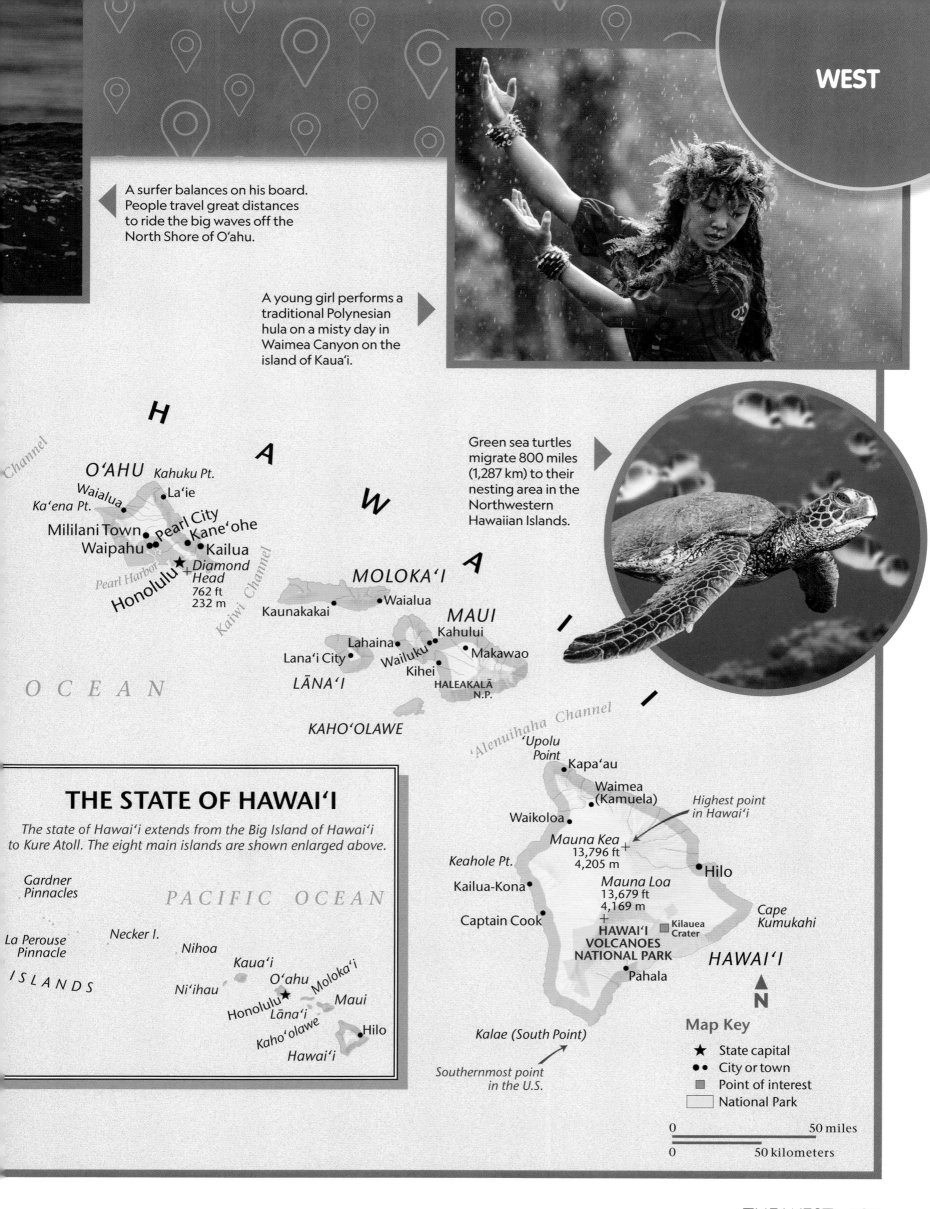

A surfer balances on his board. People travel great distances to ride the big waves off the North Shore of O'ahu.

A young girl performs a traditional Polynesian hula on a misty day in Waimea Canyon on the island of Kaua'i.

Green sea turtles migrate 800 miles (1,287 km) to their nesting area in the Northwestern Hawaiian Islands.

H
A
W
A
I
I

Channel

O'AHU   Kahuku Pt.
Waialua   • La'ie
Ka'ena Pt.
Mililani Town   • Pearl City   Kane'ohe
Waipahu   •• Kailua
Pearl Harbor   ★   • Diamond
Honolulu   Head
762 ft
232 m

Kaiwi Channel

MOLOKA'I
• Waialua

Kaunakakai •

MAUI
Kahului •
Lahaina •   • Makawao
Lana'i City •   Wailuku •
Kihei •
LĀNA'I   HALEAKALĀ
N.P.

O C E A N

KAHO'OLAWE

'Alenuihaha Channel

'Upolu
Point
• Kapa'au
Waimea
(Kamuela)
Waikoloa •   Highest point
in Hawai'i
Mauna Kea +
13,796 ft
4,205 m
Keahole Pt.   Mauna Loa   • Hilo
13,679 ft
Kailua-Kona •   4,169 m
Captain Cook •   +   Cape
HAWAI'I   Kilauea   Kumukahi
VOLCANOES   Crater
NATIONAL PARK   HAWAI'I
• Pahala

Kalae (South Point)
Southernmost point
in the U.S.

THE STATE OF HAWAI'I

The state of Hawai'i extends from the Big Island of Hawai'i to Kure Atoll. The eight main islands are shown enlarged above.

Gardner
Pinnacles

PACIFIC   OCEAN

Necker I.

La Perouse   Nihoa
Pinnacle
Kaua'i
I S L A N D S   O'ahu   Moloka'i
Ni'ihau   Honolulu ★   Maui
Lāna'i
Kaho'olawe   • Hilo
Hawai'i

Map Key

★ State capital
•• City or town
■ Point of interest
☐ National Park

N

0 ————————— 50 miles
0 ————————— 50 kilometers

IDAHO

 LAND & WATER The Bitterroot Range, the Columbia Plateau, and the Snake River are important land and water features of Idaho.

 STATEHOOD Idaho became the 43rd state in 1890.

 PEOPLE & PLACES Idaho's population is 1,754,208. Boise is the state capital and the largest city.

 FUN FACT In preparation for the first mission to the moon, U.S. astronauts visited Craters of the Moon National Monument and Preserve to study its volcanic landscapes and experience its harsh environment.

Idaho State Flag

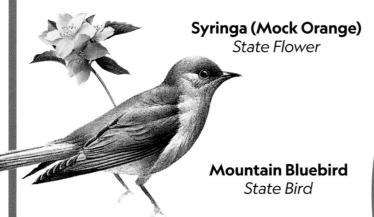

Syringa (Mock Orange)
State Flower

Mountain Bluebird
State Bird

A wood duck perches on a post. These colorful waterfowl can be viewed in Kootenai National Wildlife Refuge near Bonners Ferry.

More than 60 percent of Idaho's land area is forested. Use of this land is overseen by the Forest Products Commission in Boise. Forest products are important to the state's economy.

More than 60 percent of all potatoes grown in Idaho end up as french fries.

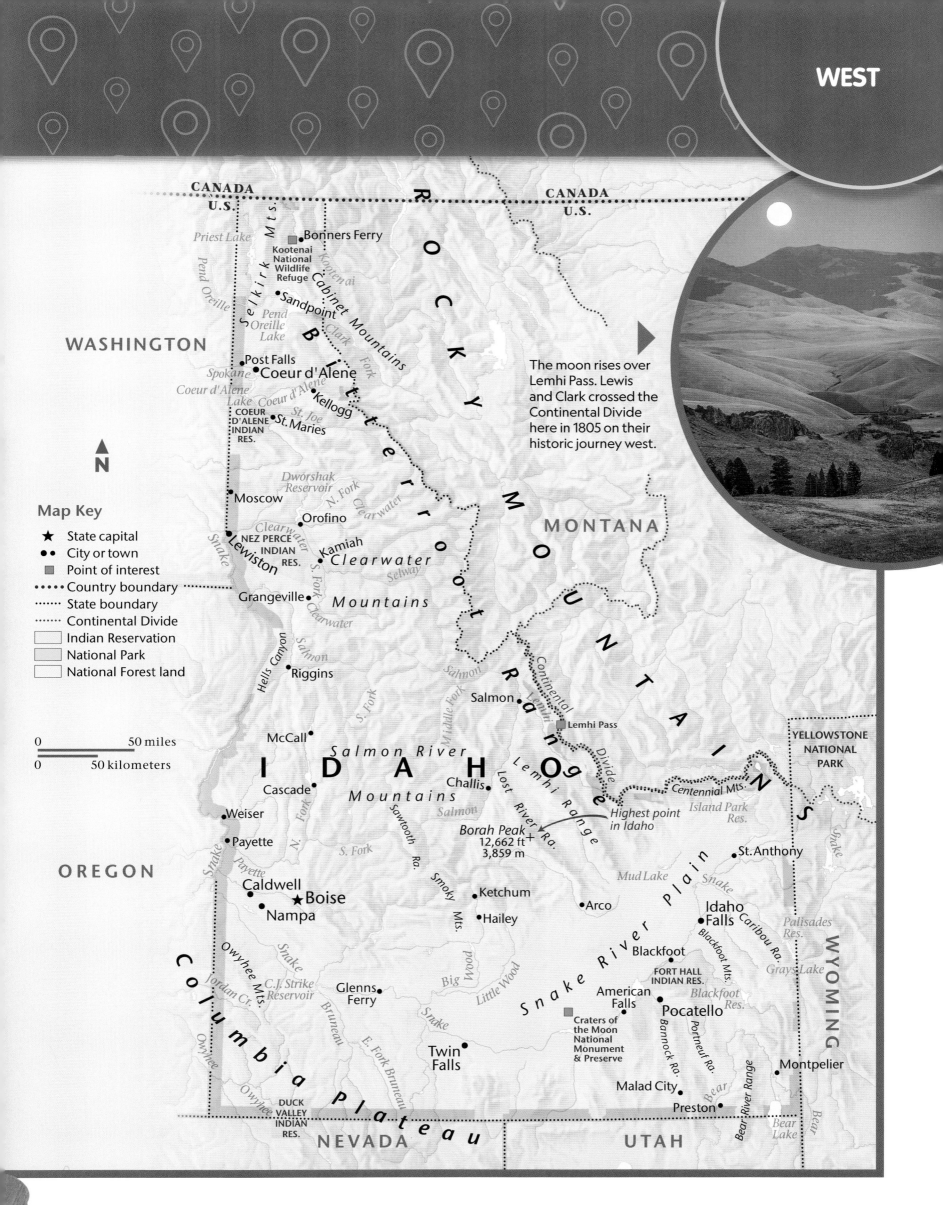

CANADA
U.S.

CANADA
U.S.

The moon rises over Lemhi Pass. Lewis and Clark crossed the Continental Divide here in 1805 on their historic journey west.

WASHINGTON

Priest Lake

◻ Bonners Ferry
Kootenai National Wildlife Refuge

Selkirk Mts.
Cabinet Mountains
Kootenai

Pend Oreille

• Sandpoint

Pend Oreille Lake

Bitterroot

Clark Fork

• Post Falls
• **Coeur d'Alene**
Spokane
Coeur d'Alene Lake
COEUR D'ALENE INDIAN RES.

Coeur d'Alene
• Kellogg
St. Joe
• St. Maries

ROCKY

Map Key

N

★ State capital
•• City or town
◻ Point of interest
•••• Country boundary
••• State boundary
••• Continental Divide
▢ Indian Reservation
▢ National Park
▢ National Forest land

Dworshak Reservoir
N. Fork
Clearwater

• Moscow
• Orofino

Clearwater
NEZ PERCE INDIAN RES.
• Kamiah
S. Fork
• **Lewiston**
Snake
Clearwater Mountains
Selway

MOUNTAINS

MONTANA

• Grangeville
Clearwater

Hells Canyon
Salmon

0 ___ 50 miles
0 ___ 50 kilometers

• Riggins
S. Fork

Salmon
Middle Fork

• Salmon
Lemhi Range
Continental Divide

◻ Lemhi Pass

RANGE

• McCall
Salmon River Mountains
S. Fork

• Challis
Lost River Ra.

Centennial Mts.

YELLOWSTONE NATIONAL PARK

I D A H O

• Cascade

Salmon

Sawtooth Ra.

Borah Peak ✛
12,662 ft
3,859 m
← Highest point in Idaho

Island Park Res.

Snake

• Weiser

N. Fork

Smoky Mts.

• Ketchum

• Arco

Mud Lake
Snake

St. Anthony •

OREGON

• Payette
Payette

• **Boise** ★
• Caldwell
• Nampa

• Hailey

• Idaho Falls

Caribou Ra.
Palisades Res.

WYOMING

Snake
Owyhee Mts.
Jordan Cr.
C.J. Strike Reservoir

• Blackfoot
Blackfoot Mts.
Grays Lake

Little Wood
Big Wood

• Glenns Ferry

FORT HALL INDIAN RES.
• American Falls

Blackfoot Res.

Owyhee
Snake
Bruneau

◻ Craters of the Moon National Monument & Preserve

• Pocatello

Bannock Ra.
Portneuf Ra.

Columbia Plateau

E. Fork Bruneau
Snake

• Twin Falls

Bear River Range

Montpelier •

• Malad City

Bear

Owyhee
DUCK VALLEY INDIAN RES.

• Preston

Bear Lake

NEVADA

UTAH

MONTANA

MONTANA

LAND & WATER The Rocky Mountains, the Great Plains, and the Yellowstone River are important land and water features of Montana.

STATEHOOD Montana became the 41st state in 1889.

PEOPLE & PLACES Montana's population is 1,062,305. Helena is the state capital. The largest city is Billings.

FUN FACT Montana is the only state with river systems that empty southeast into the Gulf of Mexico, north into Canada's Hudson Bay, and west into the Pacific Ocean.

CANADA
U.S.
Lake Koocanusa
Eureka
N. Fork Flathead
ROCKY
MOUNTAINS
GLACIER NATIONAL PARK
BLACKFEET INDIAN RES.
Browning
Continental Divide
Kootenai
Cabinet Mountains
Salish Mountains
Libby
Whitefish
Kalispell
Flathead Lake
Clark Fork
Bitterroot Range
Thompson Falls
Polson
S. Fork Flathead
FLATHEAD INDIAN RES.
Moiese
National Bison Range
Flathead
Missoula
IDAHO
Deer Lodge
Anaconda
Butte
Dillon
Red Rock
Continental

Skiers ride a chairlift up a snowy mountain slope in Whitefish.

MONTANA
ORO Y PLATA

Montana State Flag

Rugged peaks of the northern Rocky Mountains are reflected in the still surface of a mountain lake in Glacier National Park.

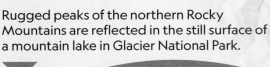

Bitterroot
State Flower

Western Meadowlark
State Bird

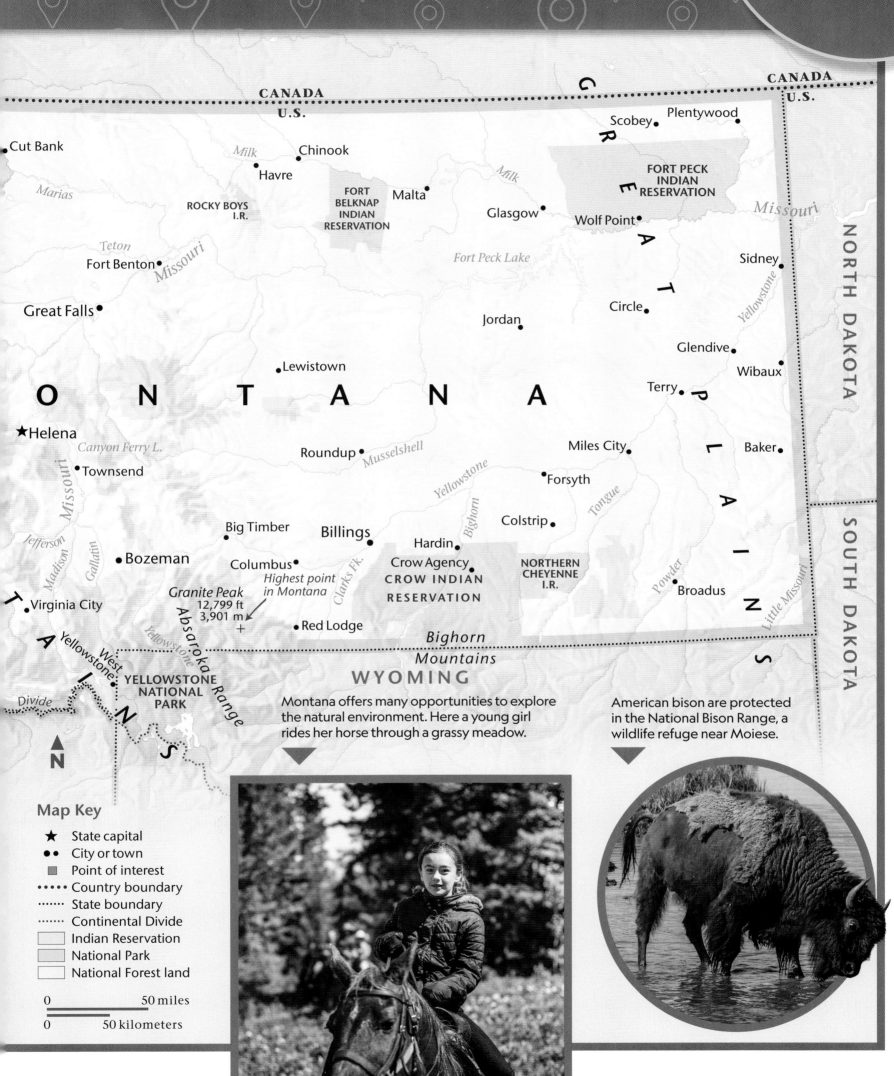

CANADA
U.S.

CANADA
U.S.

Cut Bank

Marias

Milk Chinook
Havre

ROCKY BOYS
I.R.

FORT
BELKNAP
INDIAN
RESERVATION

Malta

Milk

Scobey   Plentywood

FORT PECK
INDIAN
RESERVATION

Teton

Fort Benton

Missouri

Glasgow

Wolf Point

Fort Peck Lake

Missouri

Great Falls

Jordan

Sidney

Yellowstone

Circle

G R E A T

L E W I S T O W N

Lewistown

M O N T A N A

Glendive

Wibaux

Terry

Helena

Canyon Ferry L.

Townsend

Missouri

Roundup

Musselshell

Miles City

Baker

P L A I N S

Jefferson

Madison

Gallatin

Big Timber

Billings

Virginia City

Bozeman

Columbus

Clarks Fk.

Yellowstone

Granite Peak
12,799 ft
3,901 m
+

*Highest point
in Montana*

Red Lodge

Hardin

Crow Agency

CROW INDIAN
RESERVATION

Bighorn

Forsyth

Colstrip

Tongue

NORTHERN
CHEYENNE
I.R.

Powder

Broadus

Little Missouri

NORTH DAKOTA

SOUTH DAKOTA

T A
I N S

Yellowstone
West
YELLOWSTONE
NATIONAL
PARK

Yellowstone

Absaroka Range

*Bighorn
Mountains*

WYOMING

Divide

N

Montana offers many opportunities to explore
the natural environment. Here a young girl
rides her horse through a grassy meadow.

American bison are protected
in the National Bison Range, a
wildlife refuge near Moiese.

Map Key

★   State capital
• •   City or town
▢   Point of interest
•••••   Country boundary
······   State boundary
······   Continental Divide
▢   Indian Reservation
▢   National Park
▢   National Forest land

0   50 miles
0   50 kilometers

NEVADA

 LAND & WATER The Great Basin, the Mojave Desert, and Lake Mead are important land and water features of Nevada.

 STATEHOOD Nevada became the 36th state in 1864.

 PEOPLE & PLACES Nevada's population is 3,034,392. Carson City is the state capital. The largest city is Las Vegas.

? **FUN FACT** Kangaroo rats, which live in the Mojave Desert and other arid areas of the West, are small, seed-eating rodents that can survive with little or no water.

The Luxor re-creates a scene from ancient Egypt. It is one of the many lavish hotels that attract millions of tourists to Las Vegas.

Paiute people, dressed in ceremonial clothing, live on the Pyramid Lake Reservation near Reno. Their economy centers on recreational activities such as fishing and camping.

Nevada State Flag

The desert environment of Nevada includes many plants that tolerate very dry conditions. The setting sun highlights mountains in the distance.

Mountain Bluebird
State Bird

Sagebrush
State Flower

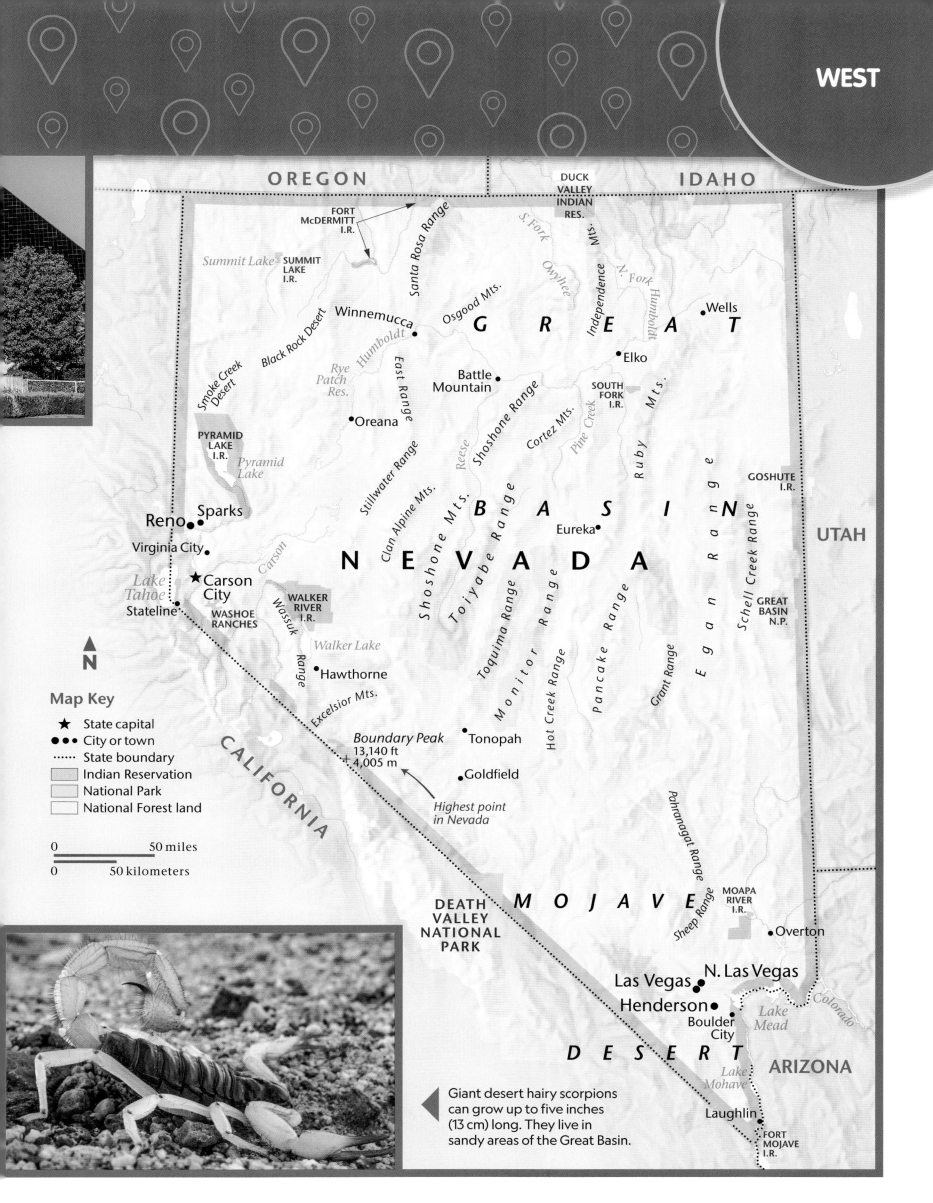

OREGON
DUCK VALLEY INDIAN RES.
IDAHO

FORT McDERMITT I.R.

Summit Lake
SUMMIT LAKE I.R.

Santa Rosa Range

S. Fork Owyhee

Independence Mts.

N. Fork Humboldt

Wells

G R E A T

Winnemucca
Osgood Mts.
Humboldt

Black Rock Desert

Smoke Creek Desert

Rye Patch Res.

East Range

Elko

Battle Mountain

SOUTH FORK I.R.

Ruby Mts.

PYRAMID LAKE I.R.

Oreana

Pyramid Lake

Stillwater Range

Reese

Shoshone Range

Cortez Mts.

Pine Creek

B A S I N

GOSHUTE I.R.

Reno
Sparks

Clan Alpine Mts.

Shoshone Mts.

Toiyabe Range

N E V A D A

Eureka

Schell Creek Range

UTAH

Virginia City

Carson

Lake Tahoe
Carson City
Stateline
WASHOE RANCHES

WALKER RIVER I.R.

Wassuk

Walker Lake

Walker Range

Monitor Range

Ruby Range

Pancake Range

Egan Range

Grant Range

GREAT BASIN N.P.

Map Key

★ State capital
●●● City or town
····· State boundary
⬜ Indian Reservation
⬜ National Park
⬜ National Forest land

Hawthorne

Excelsior Mts.

Boundary Peak
13,140 ft
+ 4,005 m

Tonopah

Hot Creek Range

0   50 miles
0   50 kilometers

CALIFORNIA

Goldfield

Highest point in Nevada

Pahranagat Range

N

DEATH VALLEY NATIONAL PARK

M O J A V E

Sheep Range

MOAPA RIVER I.R.

Overton

Las Vegas
N. Las Vegas
Henderson
Boulder City

Lake Mead

Colorado

D E S E R T

Lake Mohave

ARIZONA

◄ Giant desert hairy scorpions can grow up to five inches (13 cm) long. They live in sandy areas of the Great Basin.

Laughlin

FORT MOJAVE I.R.

OREGON

 LAND & WATER The Cascade Range, Mount Hood, and the Columbia River are important land and water features of Oregon.

 STATEHOOD Oregon became the 33rd state in 1859.

 PEOPLE & PLACES Oregon's population is 4,190,713. Salem is the state capital. The largest city is Portland.

 FUN FACT Crater Lake in the Cascade Range takes its name from the crater, or gigantic hole, created when a volcanic eruption almost 8,000 years ago caused the top of a mountain to collapse.

Oregon State Flag

Oregon Grape
State Flower

Western Meadowlark
State Bird

The 125-foot (38-m) Astoria Column near the mouth of the Columbia River is covered with scenes of historic events.

The cool, moist climate of the Willamette River Valley is well suited for growing certain varieties of grapes.

Rocky outcrops called sea stacks line Oregon's Pacific coast. They are the remains of a former coastline that has been eroded by waves.

PACIFIC OCEAN

Astoria

Trask
Tillamook

Newport

Umpqua
Coos Bay
North Bend
Coos Bay
Coos

Roseburg

Cape Blanco

Gold Beach
Grants Pass

Illinois

Brookings

COAST RANGE

WASHINGTON

Columbia

Snake

Lake Wallula

Snake

St. Helens

Hermiston

Pendleton

Columbia

Grande Ronde

Blue Mountains

Wallowa

Hillsboro Portland

The Dalles

UMATILLA
INDIAN
RES.

Beaverton Gresham

Mt. Hood
+11,239 ft
3,426 m

Highest point
in Oregon

Oregon City

Deschutes

RANGE

McMinnville

Willamette
River

WARM
SPRINGS
INDIAN
RES.

John Day

Powder

Baker
City

Salem

Albany

Willamette
River

Ochoco Mts.

John Day

IDAHO

Corvallis

McKenzie

Crooked

N. Fork

Ontario

Springfield

Bend

O   R   E   G   O   N

Malheur

Malheur

Malheur

Eugene

CASCADE

N. Umpqua

High
Desert

Burns

Harney Basin

Lake
Owyhee

Plateau

Christmas
Lake
Valley

Harney
Lake

Malheur
Lake

Owyhee

CRATER
LAKE N.P.

Crater Lake

Deepest lake in the U.S.
1,932 ft
589 m

Summer
Lake

G   R   E   A   T

S. Umpqua

Lake
Abert

Warner Valley

Steens Mountain

Owyhee

Medford

Upper
Klamath
Lake

Sprague

Ashland

Klamath Falls

FORT
McDERMITT
I.R.

Klamath

CALIFORNIA

B   A   S   I   N

NEVADA

Map Key

★ State capital

●●● City or town

•••••• State boundary

Dry lake

Indian Reservation

National Park

National Forest land

N

0   50 miles

0   50 kilometers

The climate of
Oregon is ideal
for growing fir and
spruce Christmas trees.

UTAH

LAND & WATER
The Great Basin, the Uinta Mountains, and Great Salt Lake are important land and water features of Utah.

STATEHOOD Utah became the 45th state in 1896.

PEOPLE & PLACES Utah's population is 3,161,105. Salt Lake City is the state capital and the largest city.

FUN FACT Great Salt Lake is the largest natural lake west of the Mississippi River. At its lowest water levels, the lake is as much as eight times saltier than the ocean.

Water sports such as tubing are popular activities in Glen Canyon National Recreation Area.

A newly married couple stands in front of the Temple in Salt Lake City, where Mormons gather for religious ceremonies.

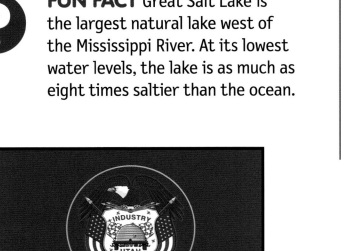

Utah State Flag

Delicate Arch in Arches National Park is one of more than 2,000 arches that have been eroded by the natural forces of wind and water over millions of years.

Sego Lily
State Flower

California Gull
State Bird

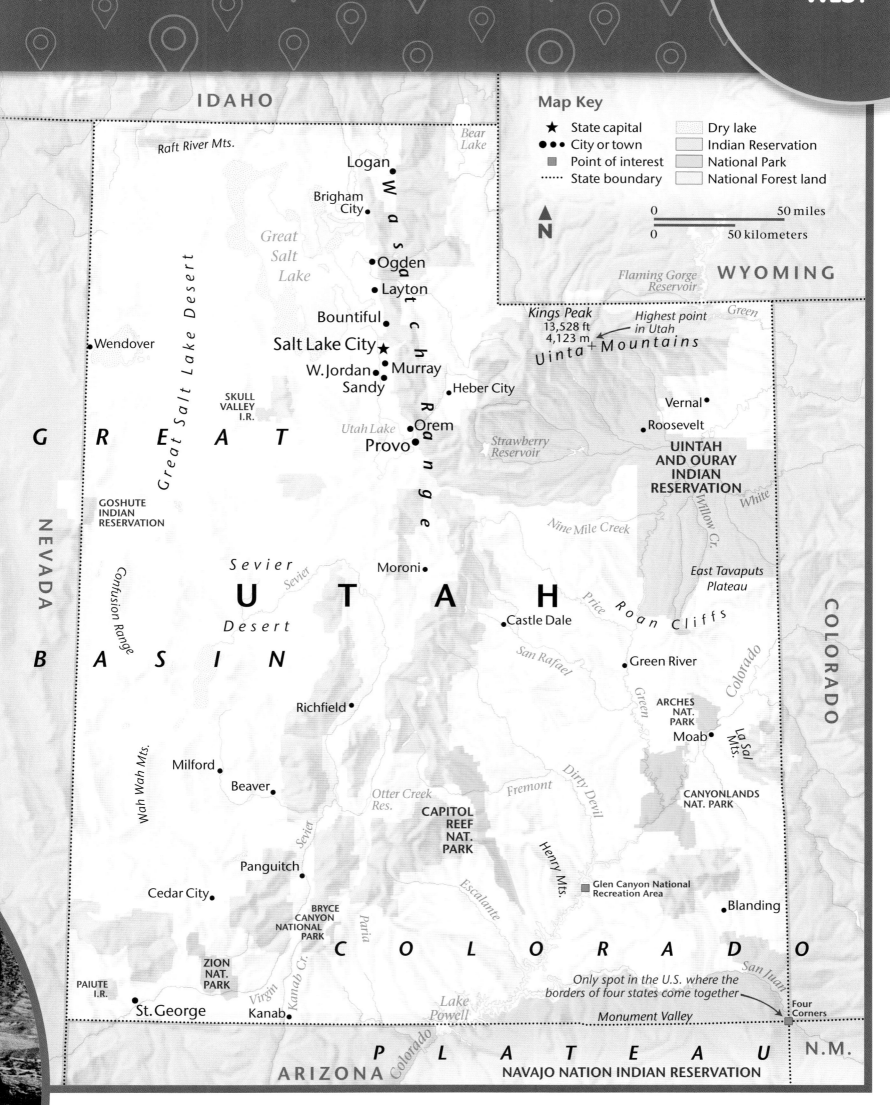

IDAHO

Map Key

★ State capital
●●● City or town
■ Point of interest
···· State boundary

Dry lake
Indian Reservation
National Park
National Forest land

N

| 0 | 50 miles |
| 0 | 50 kilometers |

Raft River Mts.

Bear Lake

Logan

Brigham City

Great Salt Lake

Ogden

Layton

W a s a t c h

Bountiful

Wendover

SKULL VALLEY I.R.

Salt Lake City ★

W. Jordan ● Murray
Sandy

Heber City

R a n g e

Utah Lake

Orem
Provo

WYOMING

Flaming Gorge Reservoir

Green

Kings Peak
13,528 ft
4,123 m

Highest point in Utah

U i n t a Mountains

Vernal ●

Roosevelt ●

UINTAH AND OURAY INDIAN RESERVATION

White

Willow Cr.

NEVADA

G R E A T

GOSHUTE INDIAN RESERVATION

Great Salt Lake Desert

Confusion Range

B A S I N

Sevier

Sevier

U T A H

Desert

Moroni ●

Nine Mile Creek

East Tavaputs Plateau

Castle Dale ●

Price

R o a n   C l i f f s

Colorado

San Rafael

Green River ●

COLORADO

Wah Wah Mts.

Milford ●

Beaver ●

Richfield ●

Green

Fremont

Dirty Devil

ARCHES NAT. PARK

Moab ●

La Sal Mts.

CANYONLANDS NAT. PARK

Otter Creek Res.

CAPITOL REEF NAT. PARK

Sevier

Panguitch ●

Cedar City ●

BRYCE CANYON NATIONAL PARK

Escalante

Henry Mts.

■ Glen Canyon National Recreation Area

Blanding ●

PAIUTE I.R.

ZION NAT. PARK

Virgin

Kanab Cr.

Paria

C O L O R A D O

Lake Powell

San Juan

Only spot in the U.S. where the borders of four states come together

Four Corners

St. George ●

Kanab ●

Monument Valley

N.M.

P L A T E A U

Colorado

ARIZONA

NAVAJO NATION INDIAN RESERVATION

WASHINGTON

WASHINGTON

LAND & WATER
The Olympic Mountains, the Palouse Hills, and Puget Sound are important land and water features of Washington.

STATEHOOD Washington became the 42nd state in 1889.

PEOPLE & PLACES
Washington's population is 7,535,591. Olympia is the state capital. The largest city is Seattle.

FUN FACT Mount Rainier, a dormant volcano, last erupted in 1969. Another nearby volcano, Mount St. Helens, erupted in 1980. Winds carried ash from the eruption as far away as Maine.

Washington State Flag

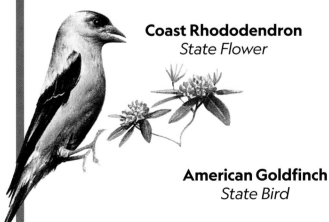

Coast Rhododendron
State Flower

American Goldfinch
State Bird

A Roosevelt elk grazes in the temperate rainforest of Olympic National Forest. Adult males weigh up to 1,000 pounds (454 kg).

The skyline of Seattle is easily identified by its Space Needle tower. The city is an important West Coast port.

Vancouver Island

Cape Flattery

Strait of Juan de Fuca

MAKAH I.R.

Port Angeles

Olympic Mountains

OLYMPIC NAT. PARK

QUINAULT INDIAN RES.

PACIFIC OCEAN

Grays Harbor

Willapa Bay

Cape Disappointment

Columbia

COAST RANGES

N

| 0 | 50 miles |
| 0 | 50 kilometers |

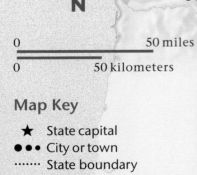

Map Key
★ State capital
●●● City or town
...... State boundary
••••• Country boundary
Glacier
Indian Reservation
National Park
National Forest land

CANADA
U.S.

CANADA
U.S.

of Georgia

LUMMI
I.R.
Bellingham

*San Juan
Islands*

NORTH
CASCADES
NATIONAL
PARK

Ross Lake

Columbia

Republic

*Franklin
Delano
Roosevelt
Lake*

Colville

Skagit

Mount
Vernon

Okanogan

Omak

Sanpoil

KALISPELL
I.R.

*Whidbey
Island*

Oak Harbor

TULALIP
I.R.

COLVILLE
INDIAN
RESERVATION

Colville

*Pend
Oreille*

Port
Townsend

Everett

*Lake
Chelan*

Skykomish

SPOKANE
INDIAN
RES.

Spokane

OLYMPIC
NATIONAL
FOREST

Kirkland

Redmond

Bellevue

Columbia

Grand Coulee

*Banks
Lake*

Spokane

Spokane Valley

Bremerton

Puget Sound

Seattle

Renton

WASHINGTON

PUYALLUP I.R.

Auburn

Tacoma

Puyallup

Wenatchee

Ephrata

Moses Lake

*Potholes
Reservoir*

Palouse

Hills

Olympia

*Mt. Rainier
14,411 ft
4,392 m*
MT. RAINIER
N.P.

Yakima

Ellensburg

*Highest
point in
Washington*

Pullman

Chehalis

Chehalis

Cowlitz

Yakima

Snake

Pomeroy

*Lake
Sacajawea*

Mount
St. Helens
8,363 ft
2,549 m

Toppenish

YAKAMA
INDIAN
RESERVATION

Richland

Pasco

Kennewick

Walla
Walla

Longview

Yakima

Prosser

Lake Wallula

C A S C A D E   R A N G E

Columbia   Plateau

Goldendale

Columbia

Blue   Mountains

Vancouver

IDAHO

Snake

O R E G O N

Tulips are big
business in the
Skagit River
Valley, where
thousands of
these colorful
flowers bloom
every spring.

An orca swims near the San Juan Islands. Also known
as killer whales, orcas live in groups called pods.

WYOMING

LAND & WATER
The Rocky Mountains, Yellowstone National Park, and the Green River are important land and water features of Wyoming.

STATEHOOD Wyoming became the 44th state in 1890.

PEOPLE & PLACES
Wyoming's population is 577,737. Cheyenne is the state capital and the largest city.

FUN FACT Wyoming is called the Equality State because it was the first state to give white women the right to vote, granted in 1869 when Wyoming was still a territory.

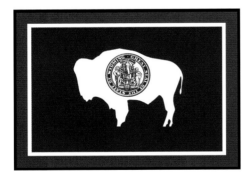

Wyoming State Flag

Indian Paintbrush
State Flower

Western Meadowlark
State Bird

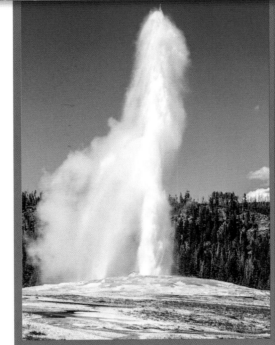

Steam and water from Old Faithful Geyser in Yellowstone National Park erupt more than 100 feet (30 m) into the air.

Map Key
★ State capital
●● City or town
■ Point of interest
······ State Boundary
······ Continental Divide
▢ Indian Reservation
▢ National Park
▢ National Forest land

```
0                    50 miles
0              50 kilometers
```

World's first national park, 1872

YELLOWSTONE NAT. PARK
Yellowstone Lake
Old Faithful

GRAND TETON NATIONAL PARK

IDAHO

Teton Range
Jackson Lake
Snake
• Jackson

Continental Divide

Wyoming Range

Lamar
Yellowstone

Bear
Green

Fontenelle Reservoir

Kemmerer • Hams Fork

Evanston •
• Lyman

UTAH

The Wyoming state capitol building in Cheyenne was completed in 1890. It is now a national historic landmark.

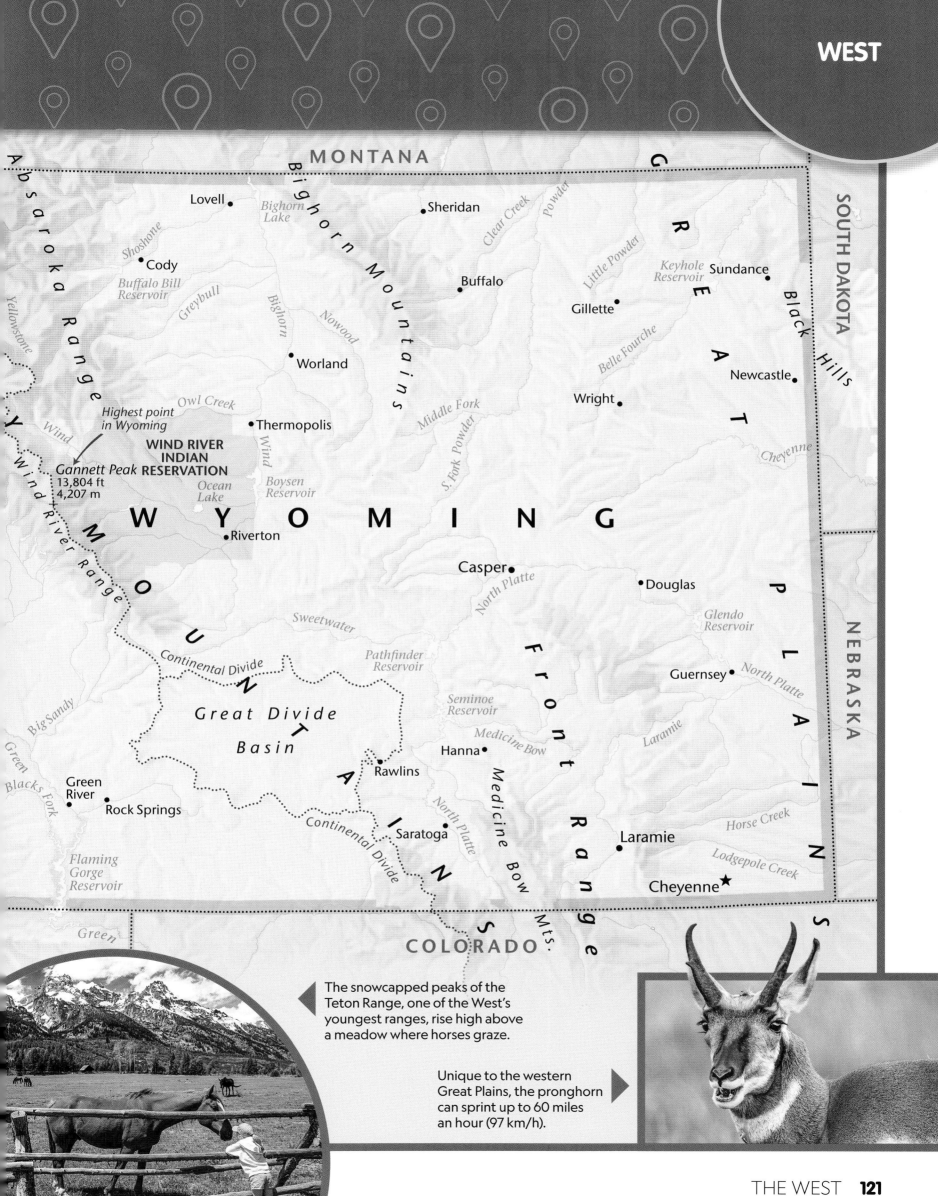

MONTANA

SOUTH DAKOTA

NEBRASKA

COLORADO

Absaroka Range

Yellowstone

Wind River Range

MOUNTAINS

Lovell

Shoshone

Cody

Buffalo Bill Reservoir

Greybull

Bighorn Lake

Bighorn Mountains

Bighorn

Nowood

Sheridan

Clear Creek

Powder

Little Powder

Buffalo

Gillette

Keyhole Reservoir

Sundance

Black Hills

Newcastle

Belle Fourche

Wright

Worland

Middle Fork

S. Fork Powder

Cheyenne

Owl Creek

Wind

Thermopolis

Highest point in Wyoming

WIND RIVER INDIAN RESERVATION

Gannett Peak
13,804 ft
4,207 m

Ocean Lake

Boysen Reservoir

W Y O M I N G

Riverton

Casper

Douglas

Glendo Reservoir

GREAT PLAINS

Sweetwater

North Platte

Continental Divide

Pathfinder Reservoir

Guernsey

North Platte

Great Divide Basin

Seminoe Reservoir

Front Range

Big Sandy

Medicine Bow

Laramie

Green

Blacks Fork

Green River

Rock Springs

Hanna

Rawlins

North Platte

Medicine Bow

Laramie

Horse Creek

Continental Divide

Saratoga

Lodgepole Creek

Flaming Gorge Reservoir

Cheyenne ★

Green

Mts.

The snowcapped peaks of the Teton Range, one of the West's youngest ranges, rise high above a meadow where horses graze.

Unique to the western Great Plains, the pronghorn can sprint up to 60 miles an hour (97 km/h).

U.S. TERRITORIES

Across Two Seas

Listed below are the five largest* of the 14 U.S. territories (areas that belong to the U.S. but that are not states), along with their flags and key information. Two are in the Caribbean Sea; three are in the Pacific Ocean. Can you find the other nine U.S. territories on the map?

U.S. CARIBBEAN TERRITORIES

PUERTO RICO

Area: 3,508 sq mi (9,086 sq km)

Population: 3,294,626

Capital: San Juan

Languages: Spanish, English

U.S. VIRGIN ISLANDS

Area: 149 sq mi (386 sq km)

Population: 106,977

Capital: Charlotte Amalie

Languages: English, Spanish or Spanish Creole, French or French Creole

U.S. PACIFIC TERRITORIES

AMERICAN SAMOA

Area: 77 sq mi (199 sq km)

Population: 50,826

Capital: Pago Pago

Languages: Samoan, English

NORTHERN MARIANA ISLANDS

Area: 184 sq mi (477 sq km)

Population: 51,994

Capital: Capital Hill

Languages: Philippine languages, Chamorro, English

OTHER U.S. TERRITORIES

Baker Island, Howland Island, Jarvis Island, Johnston Atoll, Kingman Reef, Midway Islands, Navassa Island, Palmyra Atoll, Wake Island

GUAM

Area: 217 sq mi (561 sq km)

Population: 167,772

Capital: Hagåtña (Agana)

Languages: English, Filipino, Chamorro

*Close-up views of the five largest territories are highlighted in enlarged inset maps labeled with a letter. You can see where each territory is by looking for its corresponding letter on the main map.

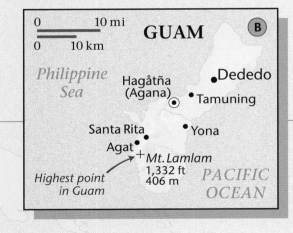

A S I A

Bering

NORTHERN MARIANA ISLANDS

Shinapaaru
Garapan • ⊙ Capital Hill
Susupe •
Saipan
Mt. Manira • *Rota*
+1,627 ft 496 m
Songsong
San Jose
Tinian
PACIFIC OCEAN
Aguijan

0   10 mi
0   10 km

MIDWAY ISLANDS (U.S.)

H A

Philippine Sea

NORTHERN MARIANA ISLANDS (U.S.)
Ⓐ ← Saipan
Rota → ← Tinian
Ⓑ GUAM (U.S.)

JOHNSTON ATOLL (U.S.)

WAKE ISLAND (U.S.)

0   10 mi
0   10 km
GUAM Ⓑ

Philippine Sea
Hagåtña (Agana) ⊙ • Dededo
• Tamuning
Santa Rita • Yona
Agat •
+Mt. Lamlam 1,332 ft 406 m
Highest point in Guam
PACIFIC OCEAN

HOWLAND ISLAND (U.S.)

BAKER ISLAND (U.S.)

AMERICAN SAMOA (U.S.)

Ofu
Tutuila → Ⓒ
Ta'ū →

PACIFIC OCEAN
NATIONAL PARK OF AMERICAN SAMOA
• Alao
Pago Pago ⊙ • Aua • Faga'itua
Fagamalo • • Fagatogo
Nu'uuli *Aunu'u*
Tutuila
• 'Āmanave
0   5 mi
0   5 km
Ili'ili
AUSTRALIA
Ⓒ
AMERICAN

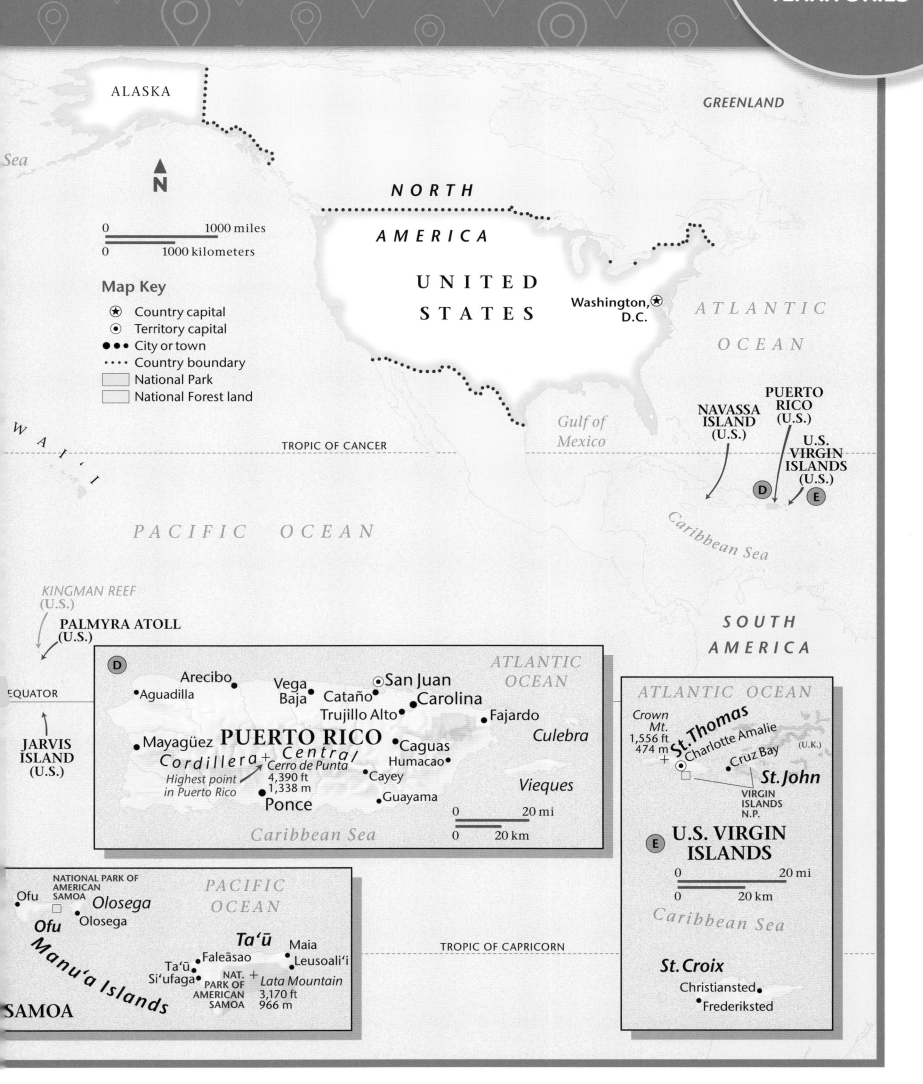

ALASKA

GREENLAND

Sea

N

0   1000 miles
0   1000 kilometers

Map Key

⊛ Country capital
⊙ Territory capital
● ● City or town
⋯⋯ Country boundary
▢ National Park
▢ National Forest land

NORTH
AMERICA

UNITED
STATES

Washington, ⊛
D.C.

ATLANTIC
OCEAN

Gulf of
Mexico

TROPIC OF CANCER

NAVASSA
ISLAND
(U.S.)

PUERTO
RICO
(U.S.)

U.S.
VIRGIN
ISLANDS
(U.S.)

D

E

H A W A I ʻ I

PACIFIC   *OCEAN*

Caribbean Sea

KINGMAN REEF
(U.S.)

PALMYRA ATOLL
(U.S.)

SOUTH
AMERICA

EQUATOR

JARVIS
ISLAND
(U.S.)

D

Arecibo
Aguadilla

Vega
Baja   Cataño

⊙ San Juan
Carolina

ATLANTIC
OCEAN

Trujillo Alto

Fajardo

Culebra

Mayagüez   PUERTO RICO
Central
Cordillera ✛ Cerro de Punta
Highest point   4,390 ft
in Puerto Rico 1,338 m

Caguas
Humacao

Cayey

Ponce

Guayama

Vieques

Caribbean Sea

0   20 mi
0   20 km

ATLANTIC OCEAN

Crown
Mt.
1,556 ft
474 m   ✛

St. Thomas
Charlotte Amalie

(U.K.)

⊙   Cruz Bay
▢   **St. John**
VIRGIN
ISLANDS
N.P.

E   U.S. VIRGIN
ISLANDS

0   20 mi
0   20 km

Caribbean Sea

St. Croix
Christiansted
Frederiksted

NATIONAL PARK
OF AMERICAN
SAMOA

Ofu ▢

Olosega
Olosega

Ofu

Manuʻa Islands

SAMOA

PACIFIC
OCEAN

Taʻū   Maia
Faleāsao   Leusoaliʻi
Taʻū
Siʻufaga   NAT.   ✛ *Lata Mountain*
PARK OF   3,170 ft
AMERICAN   966 m
SAMOA

TROPIC OF CAPRICORN

The United States at a Glance

Land
Five Largest States by Area

1. Alaska: 665,384 sq mi (1,723,337 sq km)
2. Texas: 268,596 sq mi (695,660 sq km)
3. California: 163,694 sq mi (423,966 sq km)
4. Montana: 147,040 sq mi (380,832 sq km)
5. New Mexico: 121,590 sq mi (314,917 sq km)

Water
Primary Water Bodies Bordering the U.S.

1. Pacific Ocean: 69,000,000 sq mi (178,800,000 sq km)
2. Atlantic Ocean: 35,400,000 sq mi (91,700,000 sq km)
3. Arctic Ocean: 5,600,000 sq mi (14,700,000 sq km)
4. Gulf of Mexico: 591,500 sq mi (1,532,000 sq km)

Highest, Longest, Largest

The numbers below show locations on the map.

❶ Highest Mountain
Denali (Mount McKinley), in Alaska:
20,310 ft (6,190 m)

❷ Longest River System
Mississippi–Missouri: 3,710 mi
(5,971 km)

❸ Largest Freshwater Lake
(entirely in the U.S.)
Lake Michigan:
22,300 sq mi (57,800 sq km)

❹ Largest Saltwater Lake
Great Salt Lake, in Utah:
1,700 sq mi (4,403 sq km)

❺ Northernmost Point
Point Barrow, Alaska

❻ Southernmost Point
Kalae, Hawai'i

❼ Easternmost Point
Sail Rock, West Quoddy Head, Maine

❽ Westernmost Point
Peaked Island, Alaska

People

In 2018 more than 327 million people lived in the United States. Of these, more than 44 million were born in another country. The largest foreign-born group came from Mexico, followed by India, the Philippines, and China. By 2060 it is projected that the country's population will be greater than 400 million, with almost 70 million being foreign-born.

Five Largest States by Number of People (2018)

1. California: 39,557,045 people
2. Texas: 28,701,845 people
3. Florida: 21,299,325 people
4. New York: 19,542,209 people
5. Pennsylvania: 12,807,060 people

Five Largest Cities* by Number of People (2018)

1. New York, NY: 8,398,748 people
2. Los Angeles, CA: 3,990,456 people
3. Chicago, IL: 2,705,994 people
4. Houston, TX: 2,325,502 people
5. Phoenix, AZ: 1,660,272 people

*Figures are for city proper, not metropolitan area.

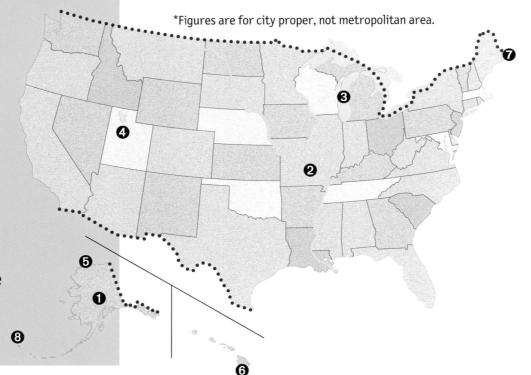

Glossary

Barrier island: a long sandy island that runs parallel to a shore

Boundary: a line on a map that separates one political or mapped area from another; physical features (such as mountains and rivers) or latitude and longitude lines sometimes serve as boundaries

Capital: a place where a country or state government is located

Central America: a region of North America (including Guatemala, Belize, Honduras, El Salvador, Nicaragua, Costa Rica, and Panama) that lies south of Mexico, joining the continents of North and South America

Coniferous forest: needleleaf trees that bear seeds in cones

Container ships: large ships that carry goods in truck-size metal containers among world ports

Contiguous U.S.: the lower 48 states, which are joined together; excludes Alaska and Hawai'i

Continental U.S.: the 49 states located on the continent of North America; excludes Hawai'i

Continental Divide: In the U.S., the natural boundary separating waters flowing into the Atlantic Ocean and Gulf of Mexico from those flowing into the Pacific Ocean

Creole: a blended language evolved from contact between two or more unrelated languages

Deciduous forest: trees, such as oak, maple, and beech, that lose their leaves in the cold season

Delmarva Peninsula: an East Coast peninsula named for the states it includes: Delaware, Maryland, and Virginia

Desert: a region with either hot or cold temperatures that receives 10 inches (25 cm) or less of precipitation a year

Dormant volcano: a volcano that is currently inactive but that may erupt at some time in the future

Erosion: the process by which wind, water, or ice carries away rocks, soil, and other weathered material on Earth's surface

Estuary: the wide part of a river near a sea, where freshwater and saltwater mix

Exports: products made in one place and sent to another to be sold

Foothills: a region of lower hills at the base of a mountain

Fossil: an impression left by the remains of ancient animals or plants that has been preserved in rock or tree sap

Grassland: large areas of mainly flat land covered with grasses

High Plains: flat or gently rolling land above 2,000 feet (600 m); semiarid region east of the Rocky Mountains

Indian reservation: land set aside by the U.S. government for Native Americans to live on and govern

Louisiana Purchase: land purchased from France in 1803 that stretched from the Mississippi River to the Rocky Mountains, and from the Gulf of Mexico to Canada, doubling the size of the country at that time

Mormon: a person who belongs to the Church of Jesus Christ of Latter-day Saints; a religion founded in the U.S. in 1830 by Joseph Smith, Jr.

Mouth: a place where a river empties into an ocean or other large body of water

Peninsula: a large piece of land that sticks out into the water

Sedimentary: a kind of rock, such as sandstone, made of small, compressed particles

Shakers: members of a religious group who did not marry and lived in communal societies

Sunbelt: a region of the southern and western U.S. experiencing rapid economic growth and population increase due to people moving to the region

Temperate rainforest: forests found along the Pacific coast of North America where there is a cool, moist climate and where rainfall is abundant

Tropical rainforest: forests near the Equator that have at least 80 inches (200 cm) of rain each year and an average yearly temperature of 77°F (25°C)

Tundra: a region at high latitudes or high elevations that has cold temperatures, low vegetation, and a short growing season

Wetland: land that is covered with or soaked by water; includes swamps, marshes, and bogs

Two-Letter Postal Codes

ALABAMA	AL	LOUISIANA	LA	OKLAHOMA	OK
ALASKA	AK	MAINE	ME	OREGON	OR
ARIZONA	AZ	MARYLAND	MD	PENNSYLVANIA	PA
ARKANSAS	AR	MASSACHUSETTS	MA	RHODE ISLAND	RI
CALIFORNIA	CA	MICHIGAN	MI	SOUTH CAROLINA	SC
COLORADO	CO	MINNESOTA	MN	SOUTH DAKOTA	SD
CONNECTICUT	CT	MISSISSIPPI	MS	TENNESSEE	TN
DELAWARE	DE	MISSOURI	MO	TEXAS	TX
DISTRICT OF COLUMBIA	DC	MONTANA	MT	UTAH	UT
FLORIDA	FL	NEBRASKA	NE	VERMONT	VT
GEORGIA	GA	NEVADA	NV	VIRGINIA	VA
HAWAI'I	HI	NEW HAMPSHIRE	NH	WASHINGTON	WA
IDAHO	ID	NEW JERSEY	NJ	WEST VIRGINIA	WV
ILLINOIS	IL	NEW MEXICO	NM	WISCONSIN	WI
INDIANA	IN	NEW YORK	NY	WYOMING	WY
IOWA	IA	NORTH CAROLINA	NC		
KANSAS	KS	NORTH DAKOTA	ND		
KENTUCKY	KY	OHIO	OH		

Metric Conversions Found in This Atlas

CONVERSIONS TO METRIC MEASUREMENTS

WHEN YOU KNOW	MULTIPLY BY	TO FIND
INCHES (IN)	2.54	CENTIMETERS (CM)
FEET (FT)	0.30	METERS (M)
MILES (MI)	1.61	KILOMETERS (KM)
SQUARE MILES (SQ MI)	2.59	SQUARE KILOMETERS (SQ KM)
POUNDS (LB)	0.45	KILOGRAMS (KG)

CONVERSIONS FROM METRIC MEASUREMENTS

WHEN YOU KNOW	MULTIPLY BY	TO FIND
CENTIMETERS (CM)	0.39	INCHES (IN)
METERS (M)	3.28	FEET (FT)
KILOMETERS (KM)	0.62	MILES (MI)
SQUARE KILOMETERS (SQ KM)	0.39	SQUARE MILES (SQ MI)
KILOGRAMS (KG)	2.20	POUNDS (LB)

Index

Pictures and the text that describes them have their page numbers printed in **bold** type.

Photo Credits

Art for state flowers and state birds by Robert E. Hynes.

COVER
Front cover: (Statue of Liberty), Amy Harris/Dreamstime; (Earth), ixpert/Shutterstock; (fireworks), yayasya/Adobe Stock; (Mt. Rushmore), EyeWire Images; (baseball), Dan Thornberg/Shutterstock; (sign), photoDISC; (eagle), EyeWire Images; Back cover: (orca), Sandy Buckley/Shutterstock; (snowboarder), Noah Clayton/Getty Images; (bear), Tony Campbell/Shutterstock; (volcano), Jim Sugar/Getty Images; (beach), Mike Brake/Shutterstock; (rocket), NASA; Front flap: (horse), Zuzule/Shutterstock

FRONT MATTER
6 (UP), Charles Krebs/Getty Images; 6 (CTR), Mike Brake/Shutterstock; 6 (LO LE), Enrique Ramos/Shutterstock; 6 (LO RT), James Randklev/Getty Images; 7, Olivier Le Queinec/Shutterstock; 8 (UP), Billy Hustace/Getty Images; 8 (LO), gurineb/Getty Images; 9 (LE), Mark R/Shutterstock; 9 (RT), dibrova/Shutterstock; 10 (UP), photoDISC; 10 (CTR), photoDISC; 11 (UP), Taylor S. Kennedy/National Geographic Image Collection; 11 (LO), Jahi Chikwendiu/The Washington Post via Getty Images

THE NORTHEAST
12, gnagel/Getty Images; 12-13, Skip Brown/National Geographic Image Collection; 14 (UP), Shawn Pecor/Shutterstock; 14 (LO RT), Donald Gargano/Shutterstock; 15, Joel Sartore/National Geographic Image Collection; 16 (UP), Jake Rajs/Getty Images; 16 (CTR), Kevin Fleming/Getty Images; 16-17 (LO RT), aimintang/Getty Images; 17, Catherine Lane/iStockphoto; 18 (UP), photoDISC; 18 (CTR), Mikael Damkier/Shutterstock; 18 (LO RT), Jeff Schultes/Shutterstock; 19, Noah Strycker/Shutterstock; 20 (UP), Emory Kristof/National Geographic Image Collection; 20 (LO RT), Veni/iStockphoto; 21 (UP), Justine Gecewicz/iStockphoto; 21 (LO), James L. Stanfield/National Geographic Image Collection; 22 (UP), Christopher Penler/Shutterstock; 22 (LO RT), Lijuan Guo/Shutterstock; 23 (LE), CO Leong/Shutterstock; 23 (RT), Brett Atkins/Shutterstock; 24 (UP), Paula Stephens/Shutterstock; 24 (CTR), Marcel Jancovic/Shutterstock; 24 (LO RT), George & Judy Manna/Getty Images; 25, Tony Campbell/Shutterstock; 26 (UP), Dave Raboin/iStockphoto; 26 (CTR), CaseyMartin/Shutterstock; 26 (LO RT), Eloi_Omella/Getty Images; 27 (UP), Andrew F. Kazmierski/Shutterstock; 27 (LO), Sheldon Kralstein/iStockphoto; 28 (UP), Cathleen Abers-Kimball/iStockphoto; 28 (LO RT), Richard Levine/Alamy Stock Photo; 29, Glenn Taylor/iStockphoto; 30 (RT), blackwaterimages/iStockphoto; 31 (LE), Jeremy Edwards/iStockphoto; 31 (RT), Racheal Grazias/Shutterstock; 32 (UP), SmarterMedium/Shutterstock; 32 (CTR), Mona Makela/Shutterstock; 32 (LO RT), Joy Brown/Shutterstock; 33, Robert Kelsey/Shutterstock; 34 (UP), Thomas M Perkins/Shutterstock; 34 (LO RT), sianc/Shutterstock; 35 (UP), Albe84/Adobe Stock; 35 (LO), rebvt/Shutterstock

THE SOUTHEAST
36, Adria Photography/Getty Images; 36-37, Maria Stenzel/National Geographic Image Collection; 38 (UP), Darryl Vest/Shutterstock; 38 (CTR), Kevin Fleming/Corbis/VCG/Getty Images; 38 (LO RT), Wayne James/Shutterstock; 39, Ronnie Howard/Shutterstock; 40 (UP), courtesy of the Museum of Discovery; 40 (LO RT), Bill Barksdale/Getty Images; 41, Travel Bug/Shutterstock; 42 (UP), Wayne Johnson/iStockphoto; 42 (LO RT), NASA; 43 (UP), Varina and Jay Patel/iStockphoto; 43 (LO), Valentyn Volkov/Shutterstock; 44 (UP), jackweichen/Shutterstock; 44 (CTR), Antonio V. Oquias/Shutterstock; 44 (LO RT), Brian Lasenby/Shutterstock; 45, Andrew F. Kazmierski/Shutterstock; 46 (UP), Leon Ritter/Shutterstock; 46 (CTR), Craig Wactor/Shutterstock; 46 (LO RT), Anne Kitzman/Shutterstock; 47, Neale Cousland/Shutterstock; 48 (UP), f11photo/Getty Images; 48 (CTR), J. Helgason/Shutterstock; 48 (LO RT), Bob Sacha/Getty Images; 49 (LE), Stephen Helstowski/Shutterstock; 49 (RT), Kathryn Bell/Shutterstock; 50 (UP), Vilmos Varga/Shutterstock; 50 (LO RT), Daniela Duncan/Getty Images; 50 (LO RT), Robert Francis/Alamy Stock Photo; 51, Mike Flippo/Shutterstock; 52 (CTR), Leah-Anne Thompson/Shutterstock; 52 (RT), Alex Krassel/Shutterstock; 53 (LE), Rob Byron/Shutterstock; 53 (RT), Brad Whitsitt/Shutterstock; 54 (RT), Rafael Ramirez Lee/Shutterstock; 55 (UP), Zach Holmes/Alamy Stock Photo; 55 (LO), Richard Ellis/Alamy Stock Photo; 56 (UP), Envision/Getty Images; 56 (LO RT), Bryan Busovicki/Shutterstock; 57 (LE), Wayne James/Shutterstock; 57 (RT), Creative Jen Designs/Shutterstock; 58 (UP), Darren K. Fisher/Shutterstock; 58 (LO RT), Travel Bug/Shutterstock; 59 (LE), Graham S. Klotz/Shutterstock; 59 (RT), Adam Kenneth Campbell/Shutterstock; 60 (UP), Robert Pernell/Shutterstock; 60 (CTR), Ken Inness/Shutterstock; 60 (LO RT), Mary Terriberry/Shutterstock; 61, Adam Kenneth Campbell/Shutterstock

THE MIDWEST
62, Holly Hildreth/Getty Images; 62-63, Jim Brandenburg/Minden Pictures; 64 (UP), Raymond Boyd/Getty Images; 64 (CTR), Tim Boyle/Getty Images; 64 (LO RT), Jenny Solomon/Shutterstock; 65, Kim Karpeles/Alamy Stock Photo; 66 (UP LE), James Steidl/Shutterstock; 66 (UP RT), Todd Taulman/Shutterstock; 66 (CTR), John J. Klaiber Jr/Shutterstock; 66 (LO RT), Melissa Farlow/National Geographic Image Collection; 68 (UP), jokter/Shutterstock; 68 (LO RT), Madeleine Openshaw/Shutterstock; 69 (LE), Steve Schneider/iStockphoto; 69 (RT), Andre Jenny/Alamy Stock Photo; 70 (UP), aceshot1/Shutterstock; 70 (LO RT), Rusty Dodson/Shutterstock; 71, Matthew/Adobe Stock; 72 (UP), Gary Paul Lewis/Shutterstock; 72 (LO RT), John Brueske/Shutterstock; 73, Cornelia Schaible/iStockphoto; 74 (UP), LazyFocus/Shutterstock; 74 (CTR), V J Matthew/Shutterstock; 74 (LO RT), Geoffrey Kuchera/Shutterstock; 75, Phil Schermeister/Corbis/VCG/Getty Images; 76 (UP), Neil Phillip Mey/Shutterstock; 76 (LO RT), Jose Gil/Shutterstock; 77 (LE), Bill Grant/Alamy Stock Photo; 77 (RT), Rusty Dodson/Shutterstock; 78 (UP), Bates Littlehales/National Geographic Image Collection; 78 (LO RT), H. Abernathy/ClassicStock/Getty Images; 79 (UP), Joel Sartore/National Geographic Image Collection; 79 (LO), marekuliasz/Shutterstock; 80 (UP), Randy Olson/National Geographic Image Collection; 80 (LO RT), CarbonBrain/Getty Images; 81, Pierrette Guertin/iStockphoto; 82 (UP), aceshot1/Shutterstock; 82 (CTR), Alex Neauville/Shutterstock; 82 (LO RT), James Marvin Phelps/Shutterstock; 83, Weldon Schloneger/Shutterstock; 84 (UP), Werner Bollmann/Getty Images; 84 (CTR), NaughtyNut/Shutterstock; 84 (LO RT), Ira Block/National Geographic Image Collection; 85, Aaron Huey/National Geographic Image Collection; 86 (UP LE), Brad Thompson/Shutterstock; 86 (UP RT), Steve Raymer/National Geographic Image Collection; 86 (CTR), Volkman K. Wentzel/National Geographic Image Collection; 86 (LO RT), Alvis Upitis/Getty Images; 87, Layne Kennedy/Getty Images

THE SOUTHWEST
88, DonLand/Shutterstock; 88-89, Jack Dykinga/National Geographic Image Collection; 90 (UP), Michael Nichols/National Geographic Image Collection; 90 (CTR), zschnepf/Shutterstock; 90 (LO RT), David Edwards/National Geographic Image Collection; 92 (UP), italianestro/Shutterstock; 92 (CTR), Mariusz S. Jurgielewicz/Shutterstock; 92 (LO RT), Ralph Lee Hopkins/National Geographic Image Collection; 94 (UP), Clint Spencer/iStockphoto; 94 (LO RT), MWaits/Shutterstock; 95 (LE), Steven Clevenger/Corbis via Getty Images; 95 (RT), Phil Anthony/Shutterstock; 96 (UP), Ben Conlan/iStockphoto; 96 (CTR), Mira/Alamy Stock Photo; 96 (LO RT), Rusty Dodson/Shutterstock; 97, CrackerClips/Getty Images

THE WEST
98, Barrett Hedges/National Geographic Image Collection; 98-99, Gordon Wiltsie/National Geographic Image Collection; 100 (UP), Benoit Rousseau/iStockphoto; 100 (LO RT), alysta/Shutterstock; 101, Michael Pemberton/Shutterstock; 102 (UP), Stas Volik/Shutterstock; 102 (CTR), PhotoviewPlus/Getty Images; 102 (LO RT), Frank Siteman/Shutterstock; 103, Elke Dennis/Shutterstock; 104 (UP), photoDISC; 104 (LO RT), Larsek/Shutterstock; 105, John P Kelly/Getty Images; 106 (UP), Jarvis Gray/Shutterstock; 106 (CTR), Jim Sugar/Getty Images; 106 (LO RT), Punchalit Chotiksatian/Shutterstock; 107 (UP), Steve Raymer/National Geographic Image Collection; 107 (LO), Jeff Hunter/Getty Images; 108 (UP), Bryan Brazil/Shutterstock; 108 (CTR), Raymond Gehman/National Geographic Image Collection; 108 (LO RT), David P. Smith/Shutterstock; 109, Dick Durrance II/National Geographic Image Collection; 110 (UP), Noah Clayton/Getty Images; 110 (LO RT), Doug Lemke/Shutterstock; 111 (LE), Dana Neibert/Getty Images; 111 (RT), Jerry Sharp/Shutterstock; 112 (UP), Andrew Zarivny/Shutterstock; 112 (CTR), W. Robert Moore/National Geographic Image Collection; 112 (LO RT), Sam Abel/National Geographic Image Collection; 113, Scott T. Smith/Alamy Stock Photo; 114 (UP), Jen Lynn Arnold/Shutterstock; 114 (CTR), Rachell Coe/Shutterstock; 114 (LO RT), Peter Kunasz/Shutterstock; 115, Lotus_studio/Shutterstock; 116 (UP), Grafton Marshall Smith/Corbis; 116 (CTR), Nelson Sirlin/Shutterstock; 116 (LO RT), PhotoDISC; 118 (UP), Natalia Bratslavsky/Shutterstock; 118 (LO RT), Luis Salazar/Shutterstock; 119 (LE), oksana.perkins/Shutterstock; 119 (RT), Sandy Buckley/Shutterstock; 120 (UP), Videowokart/Shutterstock; 120 (LO RT), Henryk Sadura/Shutterstock; 121 (LE), Peter Kunasz/Shutterstock; 121 (RT), Nancy Bauer/Shutterstock

First edition copyright © 2009 National Geographic Society
Second edition copyright © 2016 National Geographic Partners, LLC
Third edition copyright © 2020 National Geographic Partners, LLC

Published by National Geographic Partners, LLC. All rights reserved. Reproduction of the whole or any part of the contents without written permission from the publisher is prohibited.

Since 1888, the National Geographic Society has funded more than 12,000 research, exploration, and preservation projects around the world. The Society receives funds from National Geographic Partners, LLC, funded in part by your purchase. A portion of the proceeds from this book supports this vital work. To learn more, visit natgeo.com/info.

NATIONAL GEOGRAPHIC and Yellow Border Design are trademarks of the National Geographic Society, used under license.

For more information, visit nationalgeographic.com, call 1-877-873-6846, or write to the following address:

National Geographic Partners
1145 17th Street N.W.
Washington, DC 20036-4688 U.S.A.

Visit us online at nationalgeographic.com/books

For librarians and teachers: nationalgeographic.com/books/librarians-and-educators

More for kids from National Geographic: natgeokids.com

National Geographic Kids magazine inspires children to explore their world with fun yet educational articles on animals, science, nature, and more. Using fresh storytelling and amazing photography, *Nat Geo Kids* shows kids ages 6 to 14 fascinating truth about the world—and why they should care.
kids.nationalgeographic.com/subscribe

For rights or permissions inquiries, please contact National Geographic Books Subsidiary Rights: bookrights@natgeo.com

Designed by Kathryn Robbins

National Geographic supports K–12 educators with ELA Common Core Resources. Visit natgeoed.org/commoncore for more information.

Trade paperback ISBN: 978-1-4263-3825-0
Hardcover ISBN: 978-1-4263-3824-3
Reinforced library binding ISBN: 978-1-4263-3826-7

The publisher would like to thank everyone who worked to make this book come together: Martha Sharma, geographer/writer/researcher; Suzanne Fonda, project manager; Angela Modany, associate editor; Ruthie Thompson, production designer; Hilary Andrews, associate photo editor; Mike McNey, map production; Maureen J. Flynn, map edit; Joan Gossett, production editor; and Gus Tello and Anne LeongSon, design production assistants.

Printed in the United States of America
21/WOR/2